THE RELUCTANT SPY

THE RELUCTANT
SPY

MY SECRET LIFE IN THE
CIA'S WAR ON TERROR

▫ ▫ ▫

JOHN KIRIAKOU
with MICHAEL RUBY

Foreword by BRUCE RIEDEL

BANTAM BOOKS / NEW YORK

Published in the United States by Bantam Books, an imprint
of The Random House Publishing Group, a division
of Random House, Inc., New York.

BANTAM BOOKS and the rooster colophon are registered trademarks
of Random House, Inc.

LIBRARY OF CONGRESS CATALOGING-IN-PUBLICATION DATA
Kiriakou, John.
The reluctant spy: my secret life in the CIA's war on terror / John Kiriakou with
Michael Ruby; foreword by Bruce Riedel.
p. cm.
ISBN 978-0-553-80737-0
eBook ISBN 978-0-553-90733-9
1. War on Terrorism, 2001—Personal narratives. 2. Kiriakou, John. 3. Spies—United States—
Biography. 4. United States. Central Intelligence Agency. I. Ruby, Michael (Michael Handler).
II. Title.
HV6430.K57 2010   327.12730092—dc22   2009042956
[B]

Printed in the United States of America on acid-free paper

www.bantamdell.com

2 4 6 8 9 7 5 3 1

First Edition

All photographs from the author's collection

Book design by Victoria Wong

For "Katherine"
For my parents, Chris and Stella Kiriakou

FOREWORD

by Bruce Riedel

IN THE INTELLIGENCE business you learn early who you can rely on to get the job done right. John Kiriakou is one of those people. In a brilliant career he demonstrated the ability to understand what is important in confused and complex situations and how to judge information to discern how reliable and accurate it is. In this book he provides unique insights into the world of contemporary intelligence analysis and collection and into the real-world battle America is fighting against terrorism. Every American who wants to understand that battle needs to read this book; any American who wants to know what it is really like to work as an intelligence officer in the CIA should start here.

The intelligence business is a unique one. It is not a science, although it uses advanced science. As an intelligence officer, you try to peer into the future with only a few of the facts you need to see ahead. Your opponent will use deception and concealment to mislead you. You must always check and recheck your facts and your assumptions. An Israeli colleague of mine has aptly described it as more poetry than science, because those who are really good at it seem to see rhythms and patterns that are not obvious to most. In this book we see how that translates into action in the field, in trying to discern whether an enemy can be persuaded to turn sides, commit treason for our side, or provide information on what the enemy is planning. We also see how it works at headquarters where information from hundreds of sources must be deciphered, evaluated, and judged so that it can be presented to policy makers in a concise form with the insights they need to fashion our nation's future.

I first got to know John in August 1990. At the time I was deputy chief of the Persian Gulf Task Force set up in the early hours of August 3, 1990, after Iraq had invaded Kuwait. I was working without sleep for days at a time, often rushing down to the White House with the director of central intelligence to back him up at meetings of the National Security Council with President George H. W. Bush as we sought to assess Iraq's next moves from fragments of intelligence information. A relatively new officer but with expertise on Iraq and Kuwait, John was a crucial part of my team that was following the crisis around the clock from the CIA's watch office. I came to respect his judgment and knew I could rely on the analysis and information he gave me.

Our careers intersected at other times as well. We were both at the Khobar Towers in Saudi Arabia in June 1996 within hours after Hezbollah terrorists blew up a U.S. Air Force barracks and killed or wounded dozens. We both were sobered by the scene of devastation, which would be a portent of what was to come in the years ahead.

Much of the heart of this book is about the war against al-Qaeda that the CIA has been fighting since the late 1990s. Al-Qaeda is a difficult and dangerous adversary. Despite inflicting many blows on it, we have yet to destroy its top leadership, Osama bin Laden and Ayman al-Zawahiri. We squandered our best chance to do so after we had routed al-Qaeda from Afghanistan in 2001 and had them on the run in Pakistan. The capture of Abu Zubaydah that John led was one in a series of dramatic takedowns that offered the promise of getting all the way to the top.

Instead, our attention and critical intelligence resources got diverted to an unnecessary war in Iraq. John's book provides important new insights into how that happened, what it meant for al-Qaeda, and how little serious analysis was done about the implications of going after Saddam instead of Osama. There are crucially important lessons to be learned from this story about how intelligence can be misused by those in power and the costs of doing so.

John also writes in depth about the torture issue and its place in the struggle against al-Qaeda. As a country we need to get to the bottom of what happened in the CIA and in the White House regarding torture after September 11, 2001. Accountability is critical in a democracy. Our national conscience demands no less. This book is an important milestone in that process.

Espionage is a dangerous business. The terrorists have killed some of our very best officers over the past three decades. I will never forget burying one of them at Arlington National Cemetery. John's dramatic narrative reminds us that this is neither a game nor an adventure story. The men and women of the CIA who risk their lives, and sometimes the lives of their families, deserve our understanding, respect, and gratitude. Above all they deserve political leadership that puts them at risk only for good reason and asks them to uphold only the best of America.

AUTHOR'S NOTE

EVERY EMPLOYEE OF the Central Intelligence Agency agrees to submit for clearance by the agency's Publications Review Board any material he or she prepares for publication or other use in the public domain. This requirement extends to all former employees as well. The CIA also requires any author to include the following disclaimer:

> All statements of fact, opinion, or analysis expressed are those of the author and do not reflect the official position or views of the CIA or any other U.S. Government agency. Nothing in the contents should be construed as asserting or implying U.S. Government authentication of information or Agency endorsement of the author's views. This material has been reviewed by the CIA to prevent the disclosure of classified information.

This book went through several reviews by the CIA's publications board, which, to its credit, allows authors to appeal—and to continue to appeal—its demands for changes and redactions. In the end, we were required to change some names; to obscure or eliminate certain locales; and, on a few occasions, to obscure a true event or series of events. We understand the need for these changes: Much of the work of the U.S. government can and should lend itself to greater transparency. Much of what the CIA does can and should remain secret because the release of certain information could jeopardize ongoing operations or relationships or otherwise compromise U.S. national-security interests.

PROLOGUE

BOB GRENIER WAS excited, which was unusual because he was normally among the coolest of cool customers.

"John, get here as soon as you can," he said. "Something very important has come up."

It was late February 2002, and I'd arrived in Pakistan only a few weeks earlier—dispatched from CIA headquarters to become the new head of counterterrorism operations in a country with the third largest Muslim population in the world.

When I got to our offices, Grenier, the senior CIA officer in Pakistan, already had gathered a small group of FBI and CIA people to hear his news. We'd received information overnight from headquarters that Abu Zubaydah was in Pakistan. To be precise, he was in Faisalabad or one other Pakistani city.

"We've got to catch him," my boss said, looking at me, "and we want him alive."

He didn't have to say it a second time. After the mass murders of September 11, 2001, we had taken the fight to al-Qaeda in Afghanistan, with the CIA in the lead. We'd ousted the Taliban and rousted Osama bin Laden and his thugs from his stronghold in the cave complex at Tora Bora. But we hadn't captured or killed bin Laden or many of his top people, who fled to mountain villages along the Afghanistan-Pakistan border. Abu Zubaydah was part of bin Laden's inner circle, by some reckonings the number three man in al-Qaeda after Mohammed Atef was killed in Afghanistan in November 2001. He had American blood on his hands, and he could tell us plenty.

Yeah, I thought, I had to find this guy moving around two cities with a total of twenty-one million people speaking Punjabi and a bunch of other languages we didn't understand. We had fragmentary reports suggesting many locations that Abu Zubaydah or his allies might have used in Faisalabad or the other Pakistani city. But our target was smart, and he was constantly on the move.

After two weeks of frustration, I asked for help and got it when headquarters dispatched the agency's best targeting and analysis officer to Pakistan. Two days later, at 4 a.m., Rick Romanski arrived at a major Pakistani airport, managed a couple hours of sleep at a hotel, then pitched up at the office about the time the regular staff was arriving for the workday. I explained the problem to him: We knew Abu Zubaydah was in the country, and we were getting daily reports with long lists of locations and associates. But we couldn't pinpoint any locations with real certainty.

Rick got his hands on a huge piece of butcher paper, roughly the size of a U.S. billboard, pasted it up on a long wall in the office, and wrote Abu Zubaydah's name in the middle of it. As we received new reports, he would draw lines on the paper from Zubaydah's name to names and addresses of known associates in Pakistan. After a week, the paper was a beautiful mosaic, a spiderweb of lines with heavy concentrations to fourteen locations.

"These addresses are so active I can't cut any of them out," Rick told me. "I can't get the list below the fourteen"—each of them a house in Faisalabad or perhaps one other Pakistani city.

During my first month in Pakistan, we started out with practice raids on one site a night; eventually, we worked up to two sites a night—all of them targeting low-level al-Qaeda associates. Now Rick was telling me we'd have to set in motion an operation to take down fourteen sites in one night, all of them coordinated to the split second. I was going to need a much bigger team.

Fine, Grenier said when I went to him with the request. "Give me the details and a budget and I'll pass along the package to Cofer with a recommendation that he approve it." Cofer was Cofer Black, the head of the CIA's Counterterrorist Center (CTC) at Langley and one of the agency's true heroes. He came through in a big way, although the details of the package he approved remain classified.

Rick and I flew to central Pakistan, rented a suite at a hotel, and established our initial base of operations. The hotel was one of the city's finest, but it reeked of rot and mold despite the housekeepers' daily efforts to scrub everything in sight; maybe it was because they scrubbed down the carpets, too. The odor was literally breathtaking.

In a sense, the hotel was a reflection of its environment. The city suffered from desperate poverty, with twelve million people living on top of one another, pits of raw sewage along the roads, dirty air, and garbage everywhere. But the weather was good and the city overflowed with flowers, magnificent mosques, and forts dating back hundreds of years. As a result, the city even had a fairly brisk tourist industry. "Ah, yes, land of contrasts"—or so goes one of the clichés world-weary travelers use to describe such developing countries. But this huge city really was a land of contrasts, especially when compared with Islamabad—an immaculate planned city built barely a half century ago.

Rick headed back to another Pakistani city that the CIA won't allow me to name just as an Arab American CIA officer named Amir arrived. It was time to introduce ourselves to the Pakistani security authorities—specifically to a man named Khalid, who turned out to be a good guy and a team player. He'd been waiting to hear from us because his headquarters in Islamabad had already sent word to cooperate with the Americans.

"They vouch for you guys," Khalid told us. "I'll do anything you want me to do."

Khalid wasn't really cut out for security work. He clearly had other professional and even artistic interests. Even so, he and his men were terrific people—smart, cooperative, and fearless. We couldn't have asked for more.

What we really needed first, we told Khalid, was a real estate agent because we had to find a good safe house. He found a guy who showed us several houses that were either too small or too close to other houses. We required space and security. Finally, he took us to an area of the city that featured many large houses rumored to be occupied by retired military people. Big houses? These were mansions. *Either Pakistani generals receive exceptionally handsome salaries and retirement benefits,* I thought, *or they must be exceptionally corrupt.* My bet was on the latter.

Finally, the agent showed us a house with many bedrooms and bathrooms—plenty of room to accommodate us.

"How much is it?"

The agent seemed slightly embarrassed: He quoted us a figure that seemed reasonable by U.S. standards but probably was extravagant in the local real estate market.

"We'll take it," I said.

He was so flabbergasted that he didn't respond immediately. Later I learned that people generally don't pay such amounts in cash for a house with absolutely no negotiation.

Then he recovered.

"Sir, do you mind if I ask you a question?"

"No, not at all."

"What do you do for a living?"

I was tongue-tied—we'd been too busy to cook up a cover story—but Amir was nimble: "We're textile barons," he said, without missing a beat. "We own a large textile factory outside of town."

"Oh, yes," the real estate agent said, pleased with himself. "Textiles are very important to our country and employ many, many people." Then, putting his hand over his heart, he welcomed us to Pakistan.

We got a second safe house in Faisalabad because it seemed possible that all of the fourteen houses were there. The mystery, once we began to track down the locations, was site X. Most of the sites were two-room mud huts with thatched or corrugated tin roofs. Another, site Y, was a house with the shutters closed in the broiling heat; we had reports that a large group of Arabs were living there. *We'll need a big team on that one,* I thought.

Site X was on our list because Abu Zubaydah's associates had referred to it several times. But site X was nothing—or more precisely, a vacant lot.

"How can this be?" I asked the Pakistani security guy Khalid had assigned to us.

"No, no, this is common," he said. In large Pakistani cities, he explained, each plot of land is assigned a phone number, and the closest telephone pole is prewired to accommodate a line. But it's relatively easy for someone to climb the pole, splice the wire, and run a new wire to a nearby house; the charges from that line would go to the owner of the vacant land, not the telephonic thief.

The Pakistani security man got one of his young techies to the site as quickly as he could; the kid climbed the pole, started sorting through this amazing Medusa's head of wires, and finally isolated the one we wanted. On the ground, he walked the wire hand over hand down an alley. Then he stopped and pointed to an average, middle-class house. "It's that one," he said.

Amir and I smiled at each other and, this time, the words came to me first: "We got him." We were ready to go. Later, we headed out from the hotel to meet Khalid and hook up with our team at the safe house for a final briefing. Both of us were sick to our stomachs, victims of spoiled milk the hotel tea boy had inadvertently used in cappuccinos earlier in the evening. As we walked to the car, Amir wondered aloud, "So what do you think is going to happen tonight?"

I couldn't answer the question directly because I wasn't a fortune-teller. But after thinking about it, I responded as truthfully as I could.

"By this time tomorrow, we'll either be heroes or our careers will be over." In the back of my mind was an agency tour leader's remark my first week at the CIA. In the Operations Center of the original headquarters building, with its banks of television sets and clocks from around the world, he spotted a hunched older man coming out of a room and pointed at him: "See that guy? He predicted that the Israelis *wouldn't* attack in 1967. His career never recovered." Maybe it was apocryphal, but the tale resonated with me that night in Pakistan.

Our plan required coordination, but it wasn't complicated. At precisely 2:00 a.m., our teams of U.S. and Pakistani security people would use battering rams to break down doors at all fourteen locations, separate and cuff all the men, and grab everything in sight—computers, phones, weapons, documents, whatever was or wasn't nailed down. The women and children would be taken to a detention facility and released the next day.

At two o'clock Amir and I were on the roof of the Faisalabad safe house. Seconds later, we heard a sound not too far away: *boink, boink, boink*—metal on metal. "That's site X," I said, then went to our walkie-talkie. "Base to site X, come in." Nothing. Nothing a second time. Lesson learned: The first thing to fail is always communications.

I pulled out a cell phone and called the site X team leader. It turned out the door had been reinforced with steel, and they couldn't break it down. Then we heard shots.

"We got to go," I shouted to Amir.

Site X was close to the safe house, so we were there in minutes. The place was chaos, with people screaming and Pakistani security guys running everywhere. Outside the house, one man was down and obviously dead; another was gone or about to be. A third was covered in blood and screaming hysterically.

I grabbed the senior Pakistani security guy: "Where is Abu Zubaydah?"

"This is Abu Zubaydah," he said, pointing to the guy apparently close to death. The man had been shot in the thigh, groin, and stomach with an AK-47.

Amir was excited. "Oh, my God, we got him, we got him."

I wasn't so sure. "This guy doesn't look anything like his picture. Honest to God, this guy's forty pounds heavier and has this wild hair. I don't think it's him."

I called Rick and asked him what to do. "Get me a picture of his iris," he said.

"Open your eyes," I shouted at the man in Arabic, but his eyes were rolled back in his head.

"Okay, then get me a close-up of his ear." This was a new one for me: I didn't know that your ear was like a fingerprint, nearly a foolproof identification.

I photographed his ear, plugged the image into my cell phone, and sent it to Rick. A minute passed.

"It's him," Rick reported.

We got the good news to Grenier as quickly as we could. George Tenet, the director of central intelligence (DCI), had instructed Bob to let him know whether we'd been successful or not—and he wanted to know immediately. At roughly 3:45 a.m. local time, or 5:45 p.m. in Langley, Virginia, Grenier used a secure line to call Tenet, who had gathered the agency's top officials for a daily counterterrorism policy conference. Bob told me the room erupted in cheers and applause when Tenet made the announcement. Moments later, my big boss, the director, passed the word to his big boss, the president of the United States. We made a lot of people happy that night of March 28, 2002.

THE RAID IN Pakistan was one of the brightest moments of my professional life. I had joined the CIA less than two years after I completed graduate school. I wasn't exactly a choir boy, but I was a fairly provincial young man who had grown up in small-town Pennsylvania and who had few of the qualities the agency likes, especially in its covert operatives. I had no military experience and had never even touched, much less fired, a weapon. Survival skills and hand-to-hand combat were the stuff of spy novels and otherwise beyond my imagining. Foreign languages were Greek to me—

literally. It was the language of my grandfathers and became my second tongue only through diligent study in college.

I grew up in a Greek American household, with first-generation parents who were teachers and who pressed me to excel in school and extracurricular activities that, save my fixation with baseball, had everything to do with expanding my education. Love of country was a living, breathing thing in my immigrant family of FDR Democrats. At the CIA, I had signed on as an analyst in the Directorate of Intelligence, figuring that I could use my education, build upon my fascination with international affairs, particularly the Middle East, and eventually make a real contribution to the nation's understanding of the forces beyond our shores.

But I wound up spending much of my career in the Directorate of Operations—the clandestine spy service—running foreign agents, tracking down bad guys, and, yes, risking my life more times than I care to remember. We get medals and awards for this stuff, and I've got a dozen or so in a sideboard at my house, but no one does the work for honors or for personal advancement. We do it because we believe it makes our country a safer place.

The CIA became a second family—one I came to respect and even love. Too often these days, at least in the popular mind, the letters "CIA" seem to stand for cutthroat, incompetent, and addled. In fact, the agency I know is largely made up of bright, capable, patriotic people who understand the contribution they can and should be making to the nation's security as well as the limits of their mandate. Many of them are hidden heroes.

I do not wear blinders. The CIA I know can also be dysfunctional and wrongheaded in how it goes about its business. Its culture is incestuous. It is too often risk averse when it should be bold or bold when it should be cautious. Its people can be mean-spirited and vindictive, sometimes at the highest levels. I left the agency because one particular boss, a careerist with a single-minded focus on self-promotion and no regard for those crushed along the way, demanded that I make a choice between access to my young children from a first marriage and my CIA career. What choice, then, did I really have? I resigned in March 2004 after nearly fifteen years of proud service. I wasn't quite forty years old.

Every officer, I suspect, has broken the rules more than once; I know I have. These lapses are not macho badges to wear with pride. They represent situational failures of character that any officer who cares about the standards of behavior in a tough business should find deeply disturbing. My own failures in this regard trouble me to this day. But I remain proud of the vast majority of my decisions in service to my country. I chose not to participate in the agency's program to use what were called "enhanced interrogation techniques" on high-profile al-Qaeda detainees, including the man captured by the counterterrorism team I headed in Pakistan. In the spring of 2009, Americans would learn from four declassified memos what that CIA interrogation involved and determine for themselves whether we tortured in the name of national security. As a measure of the strength of our democracy, that national debate continues to this day.

Certainly in the period since September 11, 2001, American journalists and contemporary historians have cast a particularly harsh light on the CIA. Much of the criticism is probably justified. The revelations in the so-called torture memos have muted my own enthusiasm for the way the agency conducts its business. The American people want an intelligence service that serves them well and honorably and that lives up to the nation's highest values, and the CIA hasn't always delivered.

This book isn't intended to excuse the agency's shortcomings or gloss over its excesses in the post-9/11 world. It is intended as an honest account of the CIA through the eyes of a former analyst and operative whose experiences suggest that America's spy service often does a better job than the critics think.

THE RELUCTANT SPY

1

□ □ □

IT'S A REMARKABLE turn of mind in our country built upon wave after wave of immigrants: Most of us—the sons and daughters or grandchildren or great-grandchildren of foreigners—have come to take our American birthright for granted. In the land of assimilation and the melting pot, we don't spend much time puzzling over the circumstances of our citizenship or the potential consequences if our forebears had chosen a different path.

Maybe it's a Greek thing, but my heritage plays tag with my consciousness on a fairly regular basis, reminding me what might have been and how lucky I am. Yiannis Kiriakou, my paternal grandfather, was born in 1900 on the Greek island of Rhodes, then under Turkish occupation, and immigrated to the United States in 1920, when Rhodes was under an Italian thumb. It wasn't foreign occupation alone that impelled young Greeks to leave. Fighting between Greeks and Turks after World War I ended with the great population transfer, as the Turks called it, or the disaster of 1923, as the Greeks called it. Whatever it was called, the two sides expelled millions of the "others" from their lands. Greece was a mess. People were starving, there weren't enough jobs, and the government was actively encouraging young men to go abroad for work.

Yiannis, one of eighteen children, only nine of whom lived to adulthood, chose America as his destination. Other young Greeks decamped for Egypt or Lebanon, colonial capitals in Africa, reputedly untamed Australia, and the countries of South America in search of work. I have friends and acquaintances in all those places and have visited many of them for business or pleasure; with all respect, I cannot imagine any of them as home.

My grandfather boarded the SS *Themistocles*, bound for New York, mainly because an older brother, Markos, had preceded him and had set down roots in Canonsburg, Pennsylvania, eighteen miles southwest of Pittsburgh, where he worked in a steel mill. The idea was to find a job, work hard, save money, then perhaps move back to Greece and buy a farm or small business. John, my grandfather's Anglicized name in the United States, embraced this idea with a vengeance. He labored in the Canonsburg steel mill, pinched pennies, and managed to save $10,000 in a decade. That's $10,000 in 1930, the equivalent of roughly $130,000 in today's dollars. It was more than enough to buy two parcels of land on Rhodes, one a forty-five-acre farm inland, another a smaller piece on the beach. He also came into an ample dowry with his marriage to my grandmother, Ekaterini Capetan Yiorgiou—Katina for short.

The newlyweds planted olive trees and some crops on the farm and settled in for the nonce. But only eight months later, Yiannis got a letter from his brother in Canonsburg. Markos reported that the U.S. Congress was going to change the law and make it much more difficult for immigrants to become citizens. If Yiannis had any intention of bringing his bride to the United States, Markos said, he had better act immediately. My grandfather had always planned to return to America, a land he had come to love. That very day, he literally walked away from his fields and told my grandmother to pack the steamer trunks and make ready for the time of her life.

His first journey to America had been awful. The *Themistocles* was a small ship with cramped quarters on a long passage of several weeks. This time, the nearly illiterate peasant farmer would do it right. Yiannis booked first-class passage on the MN *Saturnia;* he and my grandmother arrived at Ellis Island in February 1931 and almost immediately made their way to Canonsburg, where they remained for two years before moving to Farrell, another Pennsylvania mill town. It was there in 1934, on the kitchen table of a rented house, that my father came into the world—the first Kiriakou boy born in the United States.

My grandmother Katina was an educated woman, fluent in three languages, who taught Greek and Italian for a while during the Great Depression. But for most of her life, she was a homemaker while my grandfather labored in the mill; he retired in 1965, taking over his sister-in-law's butcher shop for the rest of his working years. By that time, in the late 1960s, my own father had married, my kid brother and I had been born, and our family had moved to 307 East Fairfield Avenue in New Castle, a town about twenty miles from Farrell. That's where my two younger siblings, Emanuel and Tina, and I grew up.

New Castle, like many towns in western Pennsylvania, fell on hard times when the American steel industry got whacked by foreign competition, but in those days it was a thriving community of fifty thousand or so. In our household, education was everything. My dad, Chris Kiriakou, was a teacher and a musician with multiple degrees who eventually became an elementary school principal. He encouraged my mother, Stella, to further her education as soon as their youngest, Tina, was in kindergarten. She did, starting college when I was in fifth grade and graduating when I was a high school freshman; afterward, she got a second degree and taught school for two decades.

Both my grandfathers had been members of the United Steelworkers, and their children were union people, too—my dad in the American Federation of Musicians, my mom in the American Federation of Teachers. Kiriakou households were solidly Democratic: More than two decades after Franklin Delano Roosevelt's death, my paternal grandfather still kept a picture of FDR on top of his TV.

Because of their union backgrounds, the running conversation in the homes of my grandparents had less to do with things Greek than it did with the Depression-era politics that so profoundly influenced them. My paternal grandfather would recall attending a rally for Sacco and Vanzetti, two Italian immigrants who had been tried and executed for murder—wrongly in the view of many—in the 1920s. I was curious about these and other larger-than-life characters of his youth, and I spent time in the local library as a young teenager doing my "independent" research on their exploits.

What I discovered in the process became a lifelong passion. These men and their stories had been immortalized in song, part of a canon of folk and protest music that preceded my grandfather's arrival in America and now reaches into the twenty-first century. Greek music was omnipresent in my life, but it was the songs and ballads of people such as Woody Guthrie, honoring Sacco and Vanzetti in recordings from the mid-1940s, that captivated me with messages of revealed injustice. The television era was coming of age when I was a kid, but I was hooked on the sounds of social justice— music created by people who, in many cases, were my grandfather's chronological contemporaries. Later, when I was in college, the great Pete Seeger and a host of other folk-music icons came into my life, singing about the Big Muddy, the Swedish immigrant labor organizer Joe Hill, and more.

My grandfather also got me hooked on something else when he gave me a transistor radio. I was only eight years old, but my addiction to a technology that predated the television age by three decades began one night when I heard WGN in Chicago and thought, "Wow, if I can get a station that far away with this little radio, what can I get with a good radio?"

My father answered that question when he bought me a short-wave radio and helped me to erect a forty-five-foot tower outside our house. Suddenly, I was tuning in to broadcasts from places that were thrilling and exotic, whispering in my ear in clipped British accents on the BBC World Service or in perfect, unaccented American English on Radio Moscow. There was a separate dressing room in our old house that I converted into my "radio room." I pasted a big world map on the wall and put pins in all the countries whose short-wave stations I'd been able to verify. The alarm clock helped: I'd set it for all hours of the night so I could listen to some obscure station in Romania or the South Pacific or Africa. *Who are these people? I need to know more about them, what they look like, what they think, whether the kids are like me or different. And how different?*

School, for me, was a joy. The public elementary schools in those days were very good and New Castle High School was exceptional. We had teachers who had done things in life, who had had fascinating careers before they turned to teaching. One had been an economist, another a microbiologist with a Ph.D. Dorothy Poleno, my favorite, was a U.S. Navy intelligence officer before she retired to become a teacher. She taught a senior class called World Cultures, where we learned about the Soviet Union and its military. It was like taking a college course, with plenty of participation and interaction with the teacher.

I was active in almost everything—the American Field Service program, the debating society, the Key Club, and more—and I played baseball, my one sports passion. But it was the combination of stimulating teachers, my addiction to those radio broadcasts, and a gathering interest in politics that began to shape my future. November 4, 1979, turned out to be pivotal for me: On that day, Iranian students seized the U.S. Embassy in Tehran and held dozens of Americans hostage for what would be more than fourteen months. I was completely transfixed from the start: I listened to foreign broadcasts, read everything I could on Iran and its recent revolution, watched Walter Cronkite every night on CBS News—"And that's the way it is," followed by the date and the number of days since the hostage crisis began. I was barely fifteen years old, but there was talk of a military draft, and I wondered whether I'd be called up to go over there to free our people. The thought was at once exhilarating and frightening.

In short, I was a news junkie, even in my middle teens. There was an essay contest at school that I won, the prize for which was to become mayor of New Castle for a day. The real mayor let me sit in his chair, walked me around city hall and introduced me to all the department heads, gave me a personal tour of the city, then popped for a big working lunch—at Burger King. I asked him whether, as mayor for the day, I could fix a ticket for my dad. He said no. Then it was five o'clock and I went home.

With that I was hooked on politics, complementing my Iranian-inspired fascination with the Middle East. What sealed the deal was a one-week scholarship I won called Presidential Classroom. Two of us from my high school were selected to spend a week in Washington, D.C.—a full day at the Senate, another at the House, a third at the Supreme Court, and, of course, a tour of the White House. We joined kids from other schools and listened to speakers from government agencies—the CIA, the FBI, and the Defense Department. And we heard representatives of a labor union and a right-to-work group square off in a debate. We also met our senators and congressmen and visited both the National Cathedral and the Islamic Center of Washington. It was a fantastic hands-on week. And it convinced me that there was only one school for me: the George Washington University in the nation's capital.

I had already circled GW as a possibility, which didn't exactly thrill my father. He wanted me to go to the University of Pittsburgh, where he had studied for his Ph.D., finishing all the requirements except the dissertation—the price he paid for my birth in August 1964. Pitt, he said, had a fine Eastern European studies program; besides, it was a lot less expensive for a Pennsylvania kid than GW would be. But I didn't want to go to college only an hour away from home. And, more to the point, I was more interested in another part of the world: My major would be Middle Eastern studies, which didn't exist in the Pitt curriculum. GW was one of only a handful of schools with a quality Mideast program, I said, and it was in Washington to boot. Dad said we'd talk about it again, but he never raised it as I moved forward. I applied for early admission to GW and got applications from Georgetown and the University of Virginia as well. I was naïve: Georgetown and UVA would be my backup schools, I thought, not caring that they were more competitive than GW. In any event, my grades were good and my SAT scores were strong; GW accepted me and the other applications went into the trash can.

I was ecstatic and told Mom and Dad of my good fortune. They sure knew how to deflate a guy. They sat me down at the kitchen table and explained the financial facts of life to their eldest child. They were happy for me and very proud that I had been accepted at such a fine school, but there was no way they could afford to send me—not with tuition of $4,600 a year, plus the room and board and books and everything else. I would have to go to Pitt.

I walked away from the table like a whimpering pup whose favorite toy had suddenly been snatched away. But then I thought, *This can't be! I've got to make this work.* And I did. Before I was done, I had applied for and won more than a dozen scholarships. Many of them were small—the largest were $500 and $1,000—but they added up to enough to make tuition. I took out college loans and my aunt Chrysanthie helped, too. When I got to GW, I ended up qualifying for a half-tuition scholarship so long as my grades remained good. They did. With that, cumulative scholarships covered my tuition, room, and board—just under $8,000 a year—and a job in GW's music department covered the cost of books and incidentals.

Washington for a college student who happened to be obsessive about politics was about as close to heaven as you can get in this life. Fortunately, my roommate, Ed Harwitz, was as fanatical as I was. We bought copies of *The Almanac of American Politics* and began to digest it, one congressional district or one Senate seat per night. The next day, we'd compare notes. We also used our copies as autograph books. This was the early 1980s, when security wasn't the first order of business at the U.S. Capitol. You could walk around, buttonhole congressmen, even stroll right into the Senate cloakroom. It was amazing how few people turned us down. Ted Kennedy smiled slightly but said no, and Robert Stafford wanted to know if we were constituents. Neither one of us was from Vermont, so he just walked away. William Proxmire lived up to his reputation for crankiness and wouldn't give us the time of day. But most everyone else was approachable and cooperative: Barry Goldwater, a gem of a guy; Bob Dole, very friendly; John Glenn, just great. Glenn and Gary Hart even stood for pictures with us.

Those were the days when *The Washington Post* published a daily political calendar, listing all sorts of events, including receptions on Capitol Hill. So in our dogged pursuit of autographs, we became party crashers, too. We'd put on suits, head out, and make an evening of it. Security at these things was practically nonexistent. We'd walk in, act like we belonged, and seek out every face we recognized. Once, we spotted Al Gore and his wife, Tipper, talking to each other, with no one else around. We walked up, and I extended my hand and said, "Hey, I'm a big fan of yours. Do you mind signing our political almanacs?" Then it started to go downhill, or so I thought.

"Are you from Tennessee?"

"No, I'm from Pennsylvania."

"Aw, come on now," said Gore, who was still in the House at the time. "You're not from my state, you're not from my district, so how're you gonna vote for me if I give you my autograph?"

"Well, I can't vote for you," I said, "but I'll wish you the best of luck."

Tipper had been silent thus far, but she suddenly broke into a big smile, looked her husband in the eyes, and said, "Al, are you being an asshole?" Really, she did.

"Naw, I'm just pulling his leg," he said with a laugh. "Gimme your books, I'll sign 'em, I'll sign 'em." He not only signed them; he and Tipper even posed for a picture with us.

Our closest friends thought we were slightly loopy with all this party crashing, and they started egging us on, challenging us, I suppose, to make bigger and better fools of ourselves. We took the bait happily. After all, these receptions generally featured so-called heavy hors d'oeuvres, which meant we got free dinners two or three times a week. Once, we spotted a listing for a big bash at the Republican National Committee headquarters, and our buddies dared us to crash it. No problem, we said. But there was a problem. When we showed up, there was a guest list at the door; obviously, we weren't on it, so we improvised, using my home state's senior senator as an unwitting accessory. "Ah, well, we're from Senator Heinz's office," I said. "Has he arrived yet?" We'd scanned the room and were pretty sure he wasn't there.

"No, no, he isn't here," the gatekeeper said.

"Well, do you mind if we wait for him?"

"No, by all means, please go in."

We did. Republican parties tended to outshine the Democrats' when it came to the quality of the food. The Dems always seemed to have hot dogs and burgers or barbecue. These Republicans had sushi—by the boatload, it seemed—and champagne. We got both, moved to a big window overlooking the sidewalk, and raised flutes to our friends gathered below. Then we wolfed down the food and drink and got out before John Heinz showed up.

We were shown the door only once. We had put on our best suits and tried to crash the big dinner of a prominent political group in Washington. But we were young and white and carrying autograph books; we clearly weren't members of the Congressional Black Caucus, and the greeters at its annual banquet politely, but firmly, invited us to leave. We went quietly.

I got involved with the College Democrats, naturally, and ran the group's speakers committee. Late in 1983, I read that George McGovern was considering a run for the 1984 Democratic presidential nomination. I knew, of course, that McGovern had challenged Nixon in 1972 and had managed to win exactly one state—Massachusetts—and the District of Columbia. He couldn't even carry his home state of South Dakota. Another run would be quixotic even under the best of circumstances, but I sensed an opportunity for GW and for our College Democrats. I wrote McGovern, introduced myself, and suggested that, were he to run, the George Washington University would be a fine place to declare his candidacy. I heard nothing for a couple of weeks. Then one morning I was awakened by the phone in my dorm room. I picked it up, still groggy from sleep.

"John?"

"Yes."

"John, this is George McGovern calling."

"Oh, come on, Tom, I know it's you." My friend Tom Fitzpatrick knew I'd written McGovern and, I thought, did a pretty good imitation of the former South Dakota senator.

"No, really, this is George McGovern."

Now I was on full alert. That high nasal voice—no one could imitate that! McGovern said he'd be delighted to accept my kind offer and announce for the presidency on a stage at GW. I made all the arrangements, lured the TV networks to cover the morning event, and even got to introduce the candidate myself. Later, after the press had left, McGovern turned to me to say thanks. "You want to have lunch at my place?" he asked. So we retired to his condominium on Connecticut Avenue along with his wife, Eleanor, and daughter Mary. The candidate made the tuna fish sandwiches.

I STUCK WITH my major, Middle Eastern studies, to the mild surprise of many friends and relatives. What could be better? The region was at once rich in history and contemporary in its near-constant tension. The Iranian hostage crisis was history, but now Iran was at war with Iraq, a conflict started by the Iraqi dictator Saddam Hussein. No matter: In the Middle East, the maxim that the enemy of my enemy is my friend has special meaning, and our government was certainly leaning in Saddam's direction. Then there was the seemingly endless Arab-Israeli conflict. Egypt and Israel had signed a peace agreement in 1979, but it was a cold peace, and the region was plagued by political brushfires and worse. By the time I started at GW in late August 1982, the Israeli invasion of Lebanon was two months old. I was consumed by the subject matter, adding to the core study program all sorts of related electives—the politics and economics of oil, for example, and course work in Judaism and Islam.

A year abroad seemed like a good idea, too, and I used it as a junior at the University of London, frankly to take a break from the Middle East. I'd been working part-time at the United Food and Commercial Workers Union international headquarters in Washington my sophomore year, so I thought I'd study its counterpart—the Union of Shop, Distributive, and Allied Workers—in the United Kingdom. An InterFuture scholarship paid for the second half of an academic year; when it was over in mid-May 1985, I spent the next couple of months traveling all over Europe by train, and I made my first visit to Greece.

By the time of graduation in the spring of 1986, I had accomplished much. My knowledge in my major field of study was considerable. I had taken advantage of a program among universities in the Washington area to study Greek at Georgetown. I'd learned the language at home, but it was all slang and idiom, with no formal training. By the time I finished the two-year course at Georgetown, I was fluent.

So there I was, about to be a freshly minted graduate of the George Washington University. Okay, fine. Now what? I wasn't quite ready to face the real world yet. But I was in Washington, where politics rules and public policy occasionally counts for something, too. I was still consumed by the game and reckoned I might be able to play at a higher level. GW had an unusual three-year program at the time, offering a master's degree in legislative affairs. It seemed perfect: The reluctant undergraduate could enter graduate school and learn how the legislative sausage is made, then land a job on Capitol Hill as a top aide to a senator or House member or as a key committee staffer.

What I didn't fully understand until I started was that the

program was geared specifically to Capitol Hill staffers already several years into their careers. All the classes were held in the Hall of the States building on the Hill because it was easier for the young professionals to get from their offices to school. There were a couple of core courses on the philosophy and ethics of policy making, but most of the curriculum dealt with the arcane minutiae of the legislative process: budgetary policy making; handguns and public policy; agricultural subsidies and public policy.

GW was about three and a half miles away; to save money, I walked it most days instead of taking the Metro. I was, by a full decade, the youngest person in the program; I took classes during the summer and finished in two years instead of three. That last semester, I started to apply for jobs, shooting off résumés to the Senate foreign relations committee, the House intelligence committee, and dozens and dozens of House members and senators, especially the ones from Pennsylvania. By the time I graduated, I'd probably sent out hundreds of résumés. The other people in the program were either going back to their old jobs or parlaying their new graduate degrees into better spots in the vast network of unelected employees that make Capitol Hill function. But toward the end of that last semester, I was coming up empty and getting desperate. Finally, I accepted a position at the U.S. Office of Personnel Management as a federal investigator doing background checks on other federal employees seeking security clearances.

Then, on a May afternoon in 1988, just before graduation, one of my professors asked me to stay after class to discuss a private matter. I didn't know much about him, but I'd heard he had a big reputation as an expert in his field, and I'd certainly been impressed by what I'd seen in his class on leadership. In any event, I met with him after class, and it turned out to be the single most important meeting of my young life.

2

□ □ □

DR. JERROLD POST was a superstar at GW. He was a medical doctor specializing in psychiatry, and his principal course was on the psychology of leadership. What I didn't know was that he was also a former employee of the CIA. In the years since he left the agency, Dr. Post has appeared on many news programs as an expert in analyzing what makes various foreign leaders tick. He has been described in those interviews as one of the country's top profilers of foreign heads of state.

He asked how my job search was going.

Not so well, I told him, explaining that I was getting married in June and, because I needed income, had accepted the job at OPM.

"Well, have you ever given any thought to working at the CIA?"

"No, not serious thought." And I hadn't: I knew the CIA did analytical work, as well as all the spying, but it seemed to me as alien a government employer as NASA or the National Institutes of Health.

It turned out that Dr. Post, because of his love for the agency, tried to identify potential CIA candidates among the undergraduate and especially graduate student body at GW. He told me he'd been impressed by my analytical and writing skills in his class, and it seemed clear, he added, that I had a great interest in foreign affairs and international power politics. He didn't know whether the CIA and I would be a fit, but I was clearly interested in government service, he said, and the work at the agency might appeal to me. At a minimum, it couldn't hurt to have some preliminary conversations with CIA people.

He was right. Given my job search to date, what did I have to lose? Dr. Post picked up the phone and dialed up a guy he called Bill.

He described my academic background and said a few nice things about me, then suggested to Bill that the two of us get together.

Less than a half hour later, I was ringing the buzzer to an unmarked office in an unmarked building in suburban Virginia, just across the Potomac River. A buzzer let me in, and Bill identified himself, first name only. We chatted for twenty minutes or so—in part about me, in part about the CIA, or at least the sanitized, unclassified version of the role the agency plays in the U.S. government and in the world. He asked whether I was game to take the next step in applying for employment. "Yes," I told him.

"Can you be at the GW medical school auditorium on Saturday at eight a.m.?" The reason, he said, was a battery of tests to determine whether interested candidates would move on to the next round or be shown the door.

Perhaps two hundred people showed up that Saturday morning; the vast majority, I would learn later, had answered a CIA recruiting ad. The drill involved three tests. First, they gave each of us a map of the world that had the borders of all the countries but no names; we had to fill in the country names. A lot of people, otherwise well educated, have trouble with this kind of exercise. They tend to identify large land-mass countries easily enough—China, India, Russia—but smaller countries often trip them up. Think for a minute about the countries in Central America or parts of Africa. But I'd spent all those years as a child staring at the world map in my radio room. This was a breeze for map freaks.

Then it was on to a multiple-choice test. I still remember one question in particular: "The prime minister of Greece is (a) Andreas Papandreou, (b) U Thant, (c) Mao Tse-tung, or (d) Leonid Brezhnev." I'd had a paper route for five years as a kid and had read my product every day. And I was Greek. Still, this struck me as fairly elementary stuff for folks thinking about a career at the CIA. You didn't need to read *The Washington Post* and *The New York Times*. All you had to do is look at the front pages every day.

Finally, they gave us an extensive psychological exam. Most of the hundreds of questions were agree/disagree, such as "I like boxing." Well, I don't really have a strong position on boxing one way or the other, but there was no third option; it was either yes or no, agree or disagree. Just pencil in the appropriate circle. Okay, "I like boxing." Then, three hundred questions later, you'd get the same question again. I suppose you could have riffled back to the earlier question, but it would have been difficult, given the sea of penciled-in circles, and I didn't. It made me wonder what they learned about us from this kind of test, presumably not only from the answers but from contradictory answers. "My father was the disciplinarian in our house." Yes or no? There was no way I could screw up when that one was repeated. Answer: Yes, sir.

We had until noon, four hours in all, to finish these tests. I was done by 10:15 or so, got up, handed my booklet to the proctor, and walked out. I had absolutely no idea what to expect next.

A week later, Bill called. "Congratulations," he said. "You blew the doors off those tests." He asked whether I wanted to move forward. If so, the agency wanted to tee up a physical exam. If all was well, the physical would be followed by an interview with a team of psychologists. Actually, a psychiatrist, a psychologist, and an anthropologist, the last striking me as a curious background for a CIA evaluator. But the exercise made sense: In effect, they were asking for expanded verbal answers to some of the yes/no, agree/disagree questions in the earlier test. One of the questions that has stayed with me all these years later: "Have you ever betrayed a friendship?"

"Good lord, I hope not," I said. "I don't think so."

"We'll readdress this question on the polygraph," one of my questioners said. But it was the right answer, and "absolutely not" was not. No one could know with certainty whether a friend had ever been betrayed. Words and deeds sometimes have unintended consequences. It's the ethical intent that matters.

Two weeks later, it was time to schedule the polygraph

examination. I'd never taken a so-called lie-detector test in my life, and the prospect of one was unsettling. I called Dr. Post for some guidance; he was a psychiatrist, after all, and he probably had some experience with polygraph exams in his agency days. He was reassuring. The main thing, he said, was to try to make your mind completely blank. "Imagine you're at a drive-in theater, the movie's over, and all you see is the empty white screen. Visualize that screen and don't think about anything else." The questions would be yes or no, he said. Just answer them and you'll be fine. He also said the polygraph would probably be the last test: If you pass, you're in.

By the luck of the draw, my examiner was a thoughtful young woman who was both professional and sensitive to my visible anxiety. "I know you're nervous, just relax," she said. "I'm going to ask you some basic questions and I want you to answer me 'yes' or 'no.'" Then, she wired me up: cuffs on an arm and an ankle, some sort of belt around my stomach, little sensors on the tips of my fingers. It was like an EKG. My nervousness was showing again. "Take a minute to calm down," she said, and apparently I did.

She asked all the normal questions: Have you ever stolen anything? (No.) Did you ever take drugs? (No.) Do you have a drinking problem? (No.) Are you gay? (No.) Are you responsible with your finances? (Yes.) I sounded boring even to my ears and wondered fleetingly whether the CIA could disqualify you for terminal dullness.

I'd answered everything truthfully, but there was still a small red flag. "You're reacting to one issue," she said. "So I'm going to ask you a couple of questions again." *Oh, great, what can this possibly be? I didn't lie. Oh, God, please don't be the gay question. Please don't be the gay question.*

In fact, she said I was reacting to something about my personal finances. "My finances are an open book," I said. "I've got one credit card with no balance, a few student loans, and that's about it." She asked me a few finance-related questions and we were done.

As I was readying to leave, I asked, "How'd I do?"

"You'll get a letter from us within the next four weeks," she said—and then she winked at me. The wink was my answer: I had made it. A month later, I got a letter. The return address just said "Office of Personnel, Vienna, Virginia." I was instructed to report to CIA headquarters in Langley on such-and-such day at such-and-such time to be interviewed by three offices for a possible position.

The first was in the Directorate of Operations. The group of people interviewing me liked my background in Middle Eastern studies and that I spoke a relatively difficult language. As the interview progressed, I thought it was going well. Then one person asked me an unexpected question: "What would your wife think about spending time in a hardship post—Sudan, say, or someplace like that?" The answer to that one was as close to a no-brainer as it gets.

THROUGHOUT HIGH SCHOOL, I had never dated a Greek girl. This shouldn't have been a big deal, but our Greek American family was typical of most in America: There was incredible pressure to marry a Greek girl, and the pressure started early. By the time I was a sophomore in college, nineteen years old, Greek relatives and friends were looking for any excuse or opportunity to pair me up with this person's sister or that person's cousin. In May 1984, a friend of our family was getting married in Warren, Ohio, and naturally, we were all invited to the wedding. It was a huge affair, maybe five hundred people, Greek band, lots of liquor. Yes, just like the movie. One guy at the wedding, Victor Tsimpinos, called his younger sister and invited her to crash the party; no one would know. I knew Victor but I had no idea he had a sister until my brother, Emanuel, tapped me on the shoulder and made the introduction: "John, have you met JoAnne Tsimpinos?"

She was attractive, and we chatted for a few minutes before wandering off to talk to other people. But one of my aunts had spotted us, which was all she needed to push me to dance with my new acquaintance. JoAnne and I danced a couple of times, and I said after the last dance, "I'll give you a call sometime." Does that sound like a rock-solid commitment? Four or five days later, I got a call from a cousin, who immediately got on my case. "She's been waiting for you to call her," my cousin said. "If you tell a girl you're going to call, you should call." So I did. We dated casually until I left in January 1985 for the InterFuture scholarship, and we corresponded on a fairly regular basis while I was gone.

When I returned in July 1985, something was clearly bothering JoAnne, but I couldn't get her to say what. Instead, what I got were long, awkward silences over dinners or drinks or both. She would go silent for days or even weeks at a time, and I would have absolutely no idea what I'd done. It culminated with a scene on August 9, 1985, my twenty-first birthday, when we went out to dinner. This time, she wouldn't even make eye contact. We went to a bar afterward and it continued. Finally, I'd had enough.

"You know what? I'm taking you home. Let's go." I got up and left; she followed me out and I drove her to her house.

"Call me when you feel like saying something," I said.

"Call me when you feel like apologizing," she said. *Apologize? For what? I haven't done anything wrong. This girl has some serious issues, but they're a complete mystery to me.*

Later, I learned what the problem was. A cousin of mine said that a friend of JoAnne's was telling her that I was probably cheating on her in London because that's what all American college boys do when they go overseas. JoAnne apparently was a true believer in this breathtaking theory of social behavior. There were only two things wrong with it: First, I had made absolutely no commitment to JoAnne—no expressions of love, no physical intimacy beyond the hugs and kisses permitted by Greek dating conventions. And second, I hadn't fooled around in London anyway.

I returned to school later that August. We had no contact until the following March, when I called to wish her a happy birthday. We ended up having a couple of dates, then no contact at all until the summer of 1987, when I visited her in Warren in June. Afterward, I invited her to come to Washington over the July 4 weekend. We had a great time, taking in a concert, seeing the sights, eating at some good restaurants. Just before she was to head back, I blurted out a proposal. Just crazy. And she accepted. Even crazier.

My buddies thought I'd gone off the deep end. A close friend, Gary Senko, reminded me of the repeated fights JoAnne and I had had and how, after the big one on my twenty-first birthday, I'd asked him to stop me—"physically, if necessary"—if I ever said I wanted to get back together with her.

"No, it's okay now, she's terrific," I told him. He remained skeptical. And with good reason: We married on June 25, 1988, as I was applying to the CIA, and almost immediately started to have problems. It was the silent treatment again, punishment for imagined slights that were never explained, much less addressed. Sometimes, it would last a day or two; occasionally, a week or two would pass without our speaking more than a sentence or two to each other.

SO, A HARDSHIP post, the CIA interviewer asked. Bullshit was not an option here. I had married a Greek American princess; our marriage, if not already in trouble just four months after the exchange of vows, had more warning signs than a runaway-truck lane on a mountain pass. Making this union work would be hard enough, I sensed, even in friendly confines. Her idea of comfortable living did not include Pittsburgh or Cleveland, let alone Khartoum.

"Honestly, she wouldn't do it," I said. "I know my wife. She'd hate it."

There were a few pleasantries to follow, but not many: The interview was over.

A second interview, this one with the Directorate of Intelligence, seemed a success; they liked my academic background and the fact that Dr. Post had recommended me. But I learned later that they were oversubscribed with junior analysts and didn't feel they could take on another one.

The final interview was also in the Directorate of Intelligence, where I was asked about my favorite graduate school course. "The Psychology of Leadership," I said. That was Dr. Post's course. I must have sounded so naïve to these people; they were all Post protégés, and here I was, a Post wannabe who knew nothing of their history. I stumbled blindly on.

"This guy did a lecture on Stalin's mind-set during the Yalta Conference that I'll never forget."

"What did he say?" one of them asked. "What was it that really grabbed you?"

Dr. Post had described how Stalin had a much better understanding of Roosevelt's and Churchill's states of mind than they did of his. They underestimated Stalin, and he used that to his advantage to drive a harder bargain. Roosevelt was very ill by this time, and Stalin's insistence on meeting at Yalta, along the Black Sea, required FDR to make a long, arduous trip. Stalin also strung out the meetings, I said, parroting Dr. Post, tiring the ailing Roosevelt and the aging Churchill and making them more vulnerable to his demands. In the end, FDR may well have agreed to things he otherwise might have rejected simply to get out of the room and get some rest.

They liked what they heard, but there was one more hurdle I had to clear. They gave me a fat folder of unclassified material, most of it newspaper clips, about Benjamin Netanyahu, who had just completed a tour as Israel's ambassador to the United Nations. Take two hours, I was told, read everything, and write a two-page analytical profile that makes a prediction about Netanyahu's political future in Israel.

My prediction was that based on his political support in the Likud Party and the respect he commands among Labor Party leaders, Netanyahu almost certainly would be a leading candidate for prime minister by the mid-1990s. Netanyahu did become prime minister, a position he held from 1996 to 1999. (As of this writing, he is Israel's prime minster once again.)

My extended Greek family, in America and in Greece itself, and my travel to a few Eastern European countries after my InterFuture scholarship in London, effectively held up all my clearances as the agency checked my bona fides. Meanwhile, I labored on at OPM, patiently checking clearances for other potential federal employees and waiting to hear whether I'd made the final cut. Finally, fourteen months after the interviews at CIA headquarters, I got my offer letter from the agency.

On January 8, 1990, I walked into the building at Langley as an employee and joined the other new hires for orientation in "the Bubble," the agency's dome-shaped auditorium. We took the oath to protect and uphold the Constitution of the United States, a memorable moment that made my heart swell with love of country and pride in the government service I had chosen. A parade of speakers talked about the agency and its culture, administrative details crucial to doing our jobs, and classification rules and the proper way to lock our "vaults," the secure doors on our offices. The speaker who made the biggest impression on me, however, was the director of the Office of Security. He began by telling us how fortunate we were to be there; we were the cream of the crop, representing a mere 1 percent of all applicants. Then he said something that has stayed with me all these years later: "The greatest threat facing America today is the threat of Soviet Communism."

This was January 1990. The Berlin Wall had fallen the previous November. The Soviet empire was in collapse, with Poland, Hungary, Czechoslovakia, Bulgaria, and Romania having broken away. Germany would reunite in a matter of months, and the Soviet Union itself would be history in less than two years. Yet here was a CIA official warning us of, what? The death throes of an unlamented ideological scourge? This was something to be applauded and embraced.

It was an odd, discordant note in an otherwise thrilling day. I was about to begin work in the Directorate of Intelligence as a leadership analyst, and I was fixated on the Middle East, not the threat from an imploding empire. My first assignment: Iraq and Kuwait.

3

□ □ □

I SENT A bottle of scotch to Dr. Post as an expression of my gratitude, which seemed to embarrass him. "Nonsense," he said when we talked. "I didn't get you in, you got yourself in. I introduced you to one person. That was nothing." You could have fooled me.

A couple of years later, Dr. Post came to the agency to give a speech. Afterward, I rushed to the podium to thank him again for pointing me in the right direction. But I wasn't alone. Several other people, a few of them my contemporaries, had the same idea. We all owed our budding careers to this wonderful man and wanted to say so one more time. All the bad press notwithstanding, the CIA is filled with good men and women doing fine work on behalf of their country.

There are exceptions, of course, and one of them was my first boss when I went to work at the agency. I cannot name him here, so let's call him Jim. I was assigned to Iraq and Kuwait, Jim said, because Iraq was the perfect training account: Nothing much happened, its leadership and cabinet hadn't changed in two decades, and it was a steady state.

But what about the eight-year war Iraq had started and fought with Iran? That was a military analysis issue, Jim said. We're leadership analysis. It struck me as a distinction without a difference, especially when we were talking about Saddam Hussein, but I was a twenty-five-year-old rookie. What did I know? I figured you had to listen to the veterans if you wanted to learn more about the game. We all know what happened seven months later: Iraq invaded

Kuwait, kicking off Operation Desert Shield in early August 1990 and the Desert Storm war to remove Saddam Hussein's forces from Kuwait.

Kuwait itself was a different story, Jim said. There was an active pro-democracy movement in the emirate led in part by people who had been educated in the United States or in American universities abroad. Iraq might be quiet, but the activists in Kuwait could make trouble, Jim speculated. Could I handle both? Sure, I said, no problem.

In the spring and early summer of 1990, Kuwait was going through some internal turmoil amid efforts to bring back the National Assembly that the emir had dissolved four years earlier. A former member of that assembly was Dr. Ahmed al-Shehi. He was a real thorn in the side of Kuwait's royal family. His mother was a Sudanese slave owned by the royal family; she and his father, a Palestinian, both worked in the royal household, where young Ahmed had grown up.

Kuwait, after the discovery of oil, had more money than Croesus, so the royal family set up a scholarship fund to send Kuwaiti citizens abroad to study. Ahmed al-Shehi was the first recipient. He enrolled at the American University of Beirut, completed his undergraduate work, and entered medical school. His roommate, also studying medicine, was none other than George Habash, a firebrand who later founded the Popular Front for the Liberation of Palestine. To the extent al-Shehi needed guidance on radical politics in the region, Habash was more than happy to provide it.

I decided to write an analytical paper on al-Shehi, who had been arrested and released in May 1990. It argued that the Iraqis—by then eyeing Kuwait for a possible invasion—wanted to co-opt the Kuwaiti opposition and set up a puppet regime headed by al-Shehi. In the process, I made a modest name for myself as the go-to guy on Kuwait. And after Iraq invaded Kuwait, I became a key player in supplying analysis to policy makers in the first Bush White House straight through Operation Desert Storm. Our forces didn't go all the way to Baghdad: Taking down the regime wasn't part of the United Nations or coalition mandate, and the first President Bush wasn't about to violate it. But I figured it was only a matter of time before someone would overthrow Saddam. I wanted to be at my desk for that one; then, I'd think about moving on to something else. But Saddam hung on, even crushing uprisings among Kurds in northern Iraq and Shiites in southern Iraq. The 1992 U.S. presidential election came and went. Saddam was still in power; George H. W. Bush wasn't. With the change in administrations, I was getting antsy to try something new.

During this period, I traveled to the Middle East on business a couple of times, but only for short visits. Now, I thought I might have a shot at something more substantial. In early 1993, I applied for a position at the U.S. Embassy in Manama, Bahrain, the tiny island nation in the Persian Gulf. I got the job, as an economic officer, marking the start of a decade of work so foreign to my previous experience that I wouldn't have believed Jerrold Post himself had he been prescient enough to predict it.

Before taking the assignment, however, I had to do two things: Learn Arabic and persuade JoAnne to go to Bahrain with me. The latter may have been every bit as difficult as the former—and believe me, Arabic is not an easy language to learn. At first, JoAnne was adamant: There was no way she could do this. She had visions of being trapped in this foreign land with her young son and ambitious diplomat-husband, only worse. She was imagining scenes right out of the Sally Field movie *Not Without My Daughter.* They were going to make her wear a *hijab.* The religious police were going to smack her legs with sticks if she went out. She'd be under the equivalent of house arrest. I'd have my colleagues at the embassy, meet all sorts of interesting people in the diplomatic community, and develop a network of friends and acquaintances among the Westerners living in Bahrain. I'd do all of that and more, she said. Meanwhile, she wouldn't have any friends.

It almost broke up our marriage then and there until I effectively capitulated and gave her an out.

"Look, it won't be like that at all," I said. I had been to Bahrain once before, and I knew enough by reading what the agency had on the place to tell her that her concerns were way off base. Bahrain was a geographically small country, perhaps three or four times the size of Washington, D.C., with a population of around seven hundred thousand. It was off the coast of Saudi Arabia, connected by a four-lane causeway, but it was nothing like its huge neighbor. Bahrain, with no oil production to speak of, had turned itself into a specialist in oil services, including huge refining operations. What's more, it had become something of an international banking center. Bahrain was a Muslim country, but it was positively liberal compared with the strict Islam practiced by the Saudis. Riyadh, the Saudi capital and its largest city, was an easy drive, and Dubai and Abu Dhabi, prosperous and increasingly progressive emirates, were puddle-jumping flights away. Walking around in skintight workout clothes might be problematic, but if JoAnne dressed conservatively, she could move about freely. And she'd mix and mingle with many of the same people in my circles; she'd make friends as she saw fit. Let me put it this way: Trying to sell her on the idea, I was dancing as fast as I could.

I explained all of it to JoAnne, but she remained skeptical. "Let's make a deal here," I finally said. "At least give it a chance. If you go with me and you truly hate it, I'll send you back. Give it six weeks."

A SUCCESSFUL YEAR of Arabic study was the sine qua non of my Bahrain assignment: If I refused to commit to the language, if I washed out along the way or if I completed the year but came up short during the final testing, I'd be going nowhere. I welcomed the challenge. I'd taken a six-week Arabic course when I first joined the agency, before my first trip to the Middle East; at a minimum, I thought, a CIA guy should be able to read a street sign or a menu or even a picture caption, especially a guy with a degree in

Middle Eastern studies. But I didn't speak any Arabic, except for a few words.

So on a hot summer day in early August 1993, I began Arabic language training at a government facility in northern Virginia. Day one, however, gathered students studying all languages—scores of us—for a two-hour briefing in a language that didn't even exist in nature. This was genuine foolishness—an English-based nonsensical gibberish made up at the U.S. Defense Department's language school in Monterey, California, as a way to get some sense of our aptitude for foreign tongues. After the briefing, we were tested in a drill that reminded me of the math part of an SAT test: If you have A and B and C and D, what would come next? Verb, noun, adjective, whatever.

This was a complete waste of time. My office had mandated that I take a year of Arabic, which was the only reason for my being there, and it wasn't up to this visiting instructor from Monterey to decide whether I could cut it. Besides, I spoke fluent Greek, another language that wasn't easy to learn. I suppose I could have walked out, but I didn't; instead, I essentially blew off the test, filling in the dots at random just to finish. At the end of the day, the instructor pulled me aside with the head of the language school and said I'd done so poorly in Gibberish 101 that she was recommending that I not begin Arabic training the next morning.

"No offense, but that decision isn't yours," I said as calmly as I could. "And it's not the language school's either. My office sent me here to learn Arabic. They paid thousands of dollars for me to learn Arabic. They think I *can* learn Arabic. What you've done is flunk me in gibberish, which means you flunked me in nothing because I didn't even bother with this nonsense."

I started Arabic school the next day. There were only six of us. The two instructors sat us down, spent a few hours seeing what we knew in Arabic—the alphabet (yes), sounding out words (not really), the symbols above words (no). With two others, I was put in the beginners' class. The other three, who seemed to know a bit more, were in a slightly advanced class; they included a guy from South Carolina who knew the Arabic word for hello (*marhaba*) and began each day with a hearty, "*Marhaba,* bubba." It was funny for the first week or two; after that, he got polite, tight-lipped smiles from the rest of us, not least because he was having a hell of a time learning anything else in Arabic.

The main instructor was Ibrahim, a wonderful Egyptian guy, no longer with the agency. It was an eight-and-a-half-hour day of work, including an hour for lunch, and after the first two weeks, it was conducted entirely in Arabic. At the beginning, Ibrahim stood before us and said, "I'm going to write thirty-five three-letter verbs on this board. I need you to memorize all of them and all ten cases for each one. If you can do that by the end of the year, you're going to speak Arabic. Because everything else is going to come to you. All the other words that you're going to need to form sentences and to carry on conversations, it's all going to come to you." And he was right.

My gang of three included a fairly senior woman and a new agency hire, and we were good, all three of us. We made flash cards to test one another and read everything we could get our hands on. The instructional day began at 8 a.m., but I was so eager that I asked Ibrahim whether I could come in an hour early for a one-on-one tutorial. Sure, he said, come by at seven. I got there at 5 a.m. instead, made a pot of coffee, had a quick bite to eat, and studied until Ibrahim showed up. In effect, I was studying from 5 a.m. until 4:30 p.m. each day. In the evenings, JoAnne taught in a dance studio until 10 p.m. So I'd feed and bathe our infant, Chris, put him to bed, and study some more. Arabic newspapers. Tapes of Voice of America in Arabic. Arabic language newscasts. I'd watch *Sesame Street* in Arabic; it's an incredible tool for learning any language. My classmates were doing the same things.

There were classes in other languages at the school, of course, each one on its own timeline. By December, the people studying Spanish were already taking their final exams to test for fluency; we were just finishing the alphabet. How were we ever going to do this? They're having conversations in Spanish with university professors and we're still working on letters. There were only the two Arabic sections, of three people each, which limited interaction. This may well have slowed us down. But then we were a low-budget item on the government's shopping list for foreign-language study. Total immersion for Spanish students was a week in Mexico City; for students of German, a week in Berlin. We spent five days in Dearborn, Michigan, just west of Detroit, hanging out in its heavily Arab neighborhoods and going to a mosque where the imam lectured us on Islam in Arabic.

Our country may have had several wake-up calls in the seventies, eighties, and early nineties—an Arab oil embargo, a couple Arab-Israeli wars, intervention in Lebanon, the first Iraq war. But attention spans were limited, and apparently no one thought Arabic language study should be much of a priority—at least no one with the stroke to make it happen. We were still in a cultural Stone Age, the pre-9/11 era, when understanding Arab societies, radical Islam, and the tensions within Muslim communities didn't seem so important.

But my classmates and I were lucky: Our instructors were terrific, and Ibrahim in particular was wildly creative. He announced that it was time for a field trip—a visit to the National Zoo, where he'd teach us the names of the animals in Arabic. The next field trip was a visit to his house, where we helped him move some furniture to a rental property he'd just bought, all the time speaking nothing but Arabic. Then there were the poker games, again completely in Arabic, including one with one of the senior agency officers for Near East operations.

We were taught not merely to respond to questions with one-word answers—for example, saying "drugs" if asked to name an important problem facing the United States today. "You can't just blurt out the answer in a word," Ibrahim said. "Give the question back as part of your answer. Draw it out." Check: "In my opinion, one of the most important issues facing the United States today is the problem of illegal drug use." In these drills, Ibrahim was expanding our range in Arabic and preparing us for the forty-five-minute verbal examination that would measure our fluency—or the lack of it—at the end of our school year.

Ibrahim explained that we'd be tested at four levels of fluency. I wasn't going to make level four, but he thought that I would make level three by my exam deadline.

Level one was pretty basic. Question: "How are you today?" Answer: "I am fine, thank you."

Level two was a small step up. Question: "What's the weather like today?" Answer: "The weather today is good; it's sunny. But tomorrow will be cloudy and we may have rain."

Level two-plus represented basic conversational fluency. Question: "What's your car like?" Answer: "My car is a 1989 Volkswagen Fox. The color's red, and it's a four-door with a radio. When I get in the car, I turn on the radio and listen to the news. The car has headlights in front and yellow and red lights in the back."

Ibrahim recommended that we stretch out the answers to questions at levels one and two, demonstrating our verbal dexterity and, not coincidentally, shortening the time available for a battery of level three questions. As it turned out, I got several level three questions, but Ibrahim's preparation paid rich dividends and I handled them well, or so I thought. The two examiners, from the U.S. State Department, seemed to think so, too. Or maybe they congratulated everyone, just to hurry the process along. But about a half hour later, back in the small classroom where I'd studied for a year, Ibrahim arrived with the good news.

"Hanna," he said, using the Arabic translation of my given name before switching to the English idiom: "You sonofabitch." Then it was back to Arabic: *"Thalatha, thalatha, thalatha,"* or three, three, three—my scores for speaking, reading, and comprehension.

OUR TIME IN Bahrain wasn't an idyll, but it wasn't hard duty either. English was widely spoken in professional circles; still, I had plenty of opportunities to work on my Arabic when talking with drivers and others who provided services to the diplomatic crowd. Early on, a Bahraini driver made it painfully clear that I wouldn't be translating for the U.S. ambassador anytime soon. "You speak Shakespeare Arabic," he said with a laugh. "Nobody speaks Arabic like that." What he meant was that I had no serious training in idiomatic Arabic and, of course, no real feel for the local dialect. Even so, my basic Arabic was good, and over time, I picked up what I needed to make it better than good.

The work was interesting, and it gave me an opportunity to get a better sense of the regional economy, the oil industry and petropolitics, and the pressure points in the Islamic world. JoAnne thoroughly enjoyed the experience and left Bahrain, reluctantly, in the late spring of 1996 so that our second son, Costa, could be delivered at home. That accident of timing proved a blessing because on June 25, our eighth anniversary, all hell broke loose.

It was nearly 10 p.m., local time, about 2 p.m. in the States, and I was in our bedroom on the phone with JoAnne, wishing her a happy anniversary, saying how much I missed her and Chris, and otherwise making small talk when the front of our Bahrain house seemed to explode with a huge boom. I instinctively rolled off the bed and onto the floor, said, "I gotta go," and waited for my nerves to settle down. When I got up and moved to the front of the house, my living-room window was a mass of glass shards on the carpet. Outside, my neighbors—Americans, Brits, Germans, Swedes, and other Westerners—all thought we were under attack, but there were no craters from bombs or missiles or other signs of violence except for the massive damage to the front of our houses. I called the embassy, but at that moment, no one knew what had happened.

By morning, everyone knew. The explosion had come from Saudi Arabia, sixteen miles away. Islamic militants, taking violent exception to the continuing presence of American forces on Islam's holy ground, had blown up an eight-story building housing U.S. Air Force personnel at al-Khobar, killing nineteen. I knew exactly where al Khobar was: From my front yard, you could see its lights across the waters of the Persian Gulf. I wasn't surprised when my superior in Bahrain told me to report to Ambassador David Ransom. Ransom, a former U.S. marine who died in 2003, was a fine man, but I wasn't thrilled with the message that morning.

"Do you have a Saudi visa?"

"Yes, sir."

"Do you think you can go over there and help them with this Khobar Towers bombing?"

"Yes, sir." *Oh, brother, Saudi Arabia is the last frigging place I want to be today.*

"Can you leave in twenty minutes?" Ransom asked.

"Yes, sir."

Two of us from the embassy in Bahrain jumped into a car and drove across the causeway as quickly as we could. The scene at al-Khobar was horrific. The bomb must have been massive because it left a crater thirty feet deep, and water was seeping into it from the Gulf. The façade of the building was sheared off, and the furniture had either been vaporized or blown to bits. But there were mattresses everywhere, and when you looked up into this shell of a building, you could see huge bloodstains streaking the apartment ceilings. People had been blown out of their beds, and the force of the blast crushed them against the next surface they encountered. It was a miracle the death count wasn't much higher.

By coincidence, Secretary of State Warren Christopher and State's chief spokesman, Nicholas Burns, were in Cairo on a diplomatic trip, accompanied by a CNN crew. After the bombing, they immediately flew to Saudi Arabia. My job was to make sure that Christopher, Burns, and CNN got to a certain palace to meet Prince Muhammad al-Saud, the governor of the Saudi Eastern Province. Then I had to get them to the TV station in Dhahran so they could do their interviews. It was my first encounter with Burns, who would rise to become undersecretary of state for political affairs during George W. Bush's second term. Unfortunately, it wouldn't be my last.

I LEFT BAHRAIN at the end of July 1996, my two-year temporary assignment over. It had ended with a vivid and tragic reminder of why the Middle East fascinated me. Our scholars in academia and our analysts in government knew so much—and yet most of them had failed to appreciate fully the strength of a new and dangerous force growing and metastasizing in certain parts of the Arab and Muslim world. Two months earlier, having been booted from Sudan, Osama bin Laden had returned to Afghanistan, where he had fought to expel the Soviets in the 1980s and where he now made common cause with Mullah Omar and his Taliban thugs. We would hear more from these lunatics soon enough.

Back at Langley, I began work as a political analyst, supposedly specializing in Iraq. But not quite yet, the bosses said; we're short-handed and we need you to fill in for three months on a familiar account: Bahrain, Kuwait, and Qatar. What the hell, I was a good soldier. I saluted and said yes. But three months became six months, then nine months, with no winks or nods hinting at an end in sight. The bosses liked my work, and there weren't a bunch of eager beavers gnawing trees to replace me. It was clear, to me at least, that I could grow very old in this particular job unless I made them live up to their earlier promise. Enough, I said. Either put me on Iraq or

I'll have to start looking for work outside the office. It took another couple of months, but they finally delivered.

I started working on Iraq in July 1997 and was told early on that I'd have to write an important analytical paper if I wanted to be promoted. Fair enough, I said, what do you have in mind? Nothing less than a National Intelligence Estimate, my boss said. Samuel R. "Sandy" Berger, President Clinton's national security adviser, wanted an NIE that would examine Saddam's likely intentions over the next year.

An NIE is a big deal; it's supposed to represent the collective wisdom of the so-called intelligence community—not only the CIA, but the intelligence arms of the military services, the National Security Agency, and others. This was an opportunity to make a real name for myself, and I felt fairly confident going in, figuring I knew as much about Iraq as anybody in the intelligence community. So I wrote a paper that said Iraq could violate the no-fly zone, threaten the Shiites, threaten the Kurds, threaten Kuwait, continue to provoke us militarily, and continue to violate sanctions. But when I was done and reread my work, I thought, *This is the worst analytical paper I've ever written. This is exactly what we've said every year for the past five years. There's absolutely nothing new here.*

By that time, however, there was no turning back. Ben Bonk, the national intelligence officer covering the Middle East at the time, had already told the sixteen different services of the intelligence community that the document was coming. Ben convened a meeting, and it took four hours for this Gang of Sixteen to agree on my language. Afterward, Ben congratulated me.

"That was the fastest NIE coordination meeting I've ever been through."

"Ben, I'm embarrassed by this paper. We didn't say anything new at all. There are no bold predictions, nothing. It's like we just took last year's paper and changed the date." *They're going to see this crap in the White House and wonder about the idiot at Langley who produced it. So ends the short happy career of the Greek kid from New Castle, Pennsylvania.*

Off it went to Berger. Two weeks later, the word came down: Berger loved the paper. It was exactly what he was looking for.

Fine, but did it take this formal duty dance to make the point that Saddam was a continuing source of instability in the region? From my perspective, it looked like a classic cover-your-ass exercise. Chalk one up for my learning curve.

4

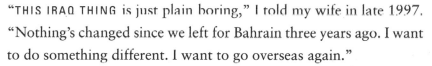

"THIS IRAQ THING is just plain boring," I told my wife in late 1997. "Nothing's changed since we left for Bahrain three years ago. I want to do something different. I want to go overseas again."

There it was, out on the table. Even if the Iraq account had stimulated every intellectual neuron in my brain pan, I hankered for an assignment abroad. Bahrain, a tame posting until the end, had planted a seed. I spoke a couple of difficult foreign languages; I had studied the Middle East, and I thought I understood the issues and threats confronting my country in some of the most dangerous neighborhoods of the world. It was where I could make a bigger contribution and, not coincidentally, test myself in employing skills I'd only read about in books.

JoAnne was even more skeptical than she was before Bahrain, which struck me as odd, given the happy days she had spent there even by her own admission. I guess it was because she didn't think lightning could strike twice. "The only place I'd go is Athens," she said. Well, of course: She was a good Greek American girl with extended family ties in the old country—in effect, a ready-made support system of relatives and friends of relatives who would embrace her and make her feel as if she'd never left Warren, Ohio. Amazingly, Athens wasn't out of the question. The agency was seeking an officer for a special counterterrorism program; the right candidate would take specific assignments in Greece, Italy, Bulgaria, Romania, and elsewhere in southern and eastern Europe, focusing on militant leftist and Arab terrorist groups in the region. If possible, the pooh-bahs wanted someone who spoke Arabic as well as Greek. It was almost as if they were designing the assignment with me in mind, except for one rather important omission on my résumé.

I went to see Dan Praig, the official in the Counterterrorist Center responsible for filling the post, and introduced myself.

"Look, I've got to tell you up front, I don't have any operational experience at all." I told Praig what I had done as an analyst, but that I had never been in the field as a covert operative.

Praig paused, frowning slightly, and I jumped back in. "But listen, I speak Greek and Arabic fluently."

"You what? Greek and Arabic? You willing to be tested?"

"Absolutely," I said.

It turned out Praig's secretary was a Greek immigrant whose brother lived on Rhodes, the island my grandparents came from. A nod from Praig, and she immediately started talking to me in rapid-fire Greek; in no time, the two of us got right into a conversation, complete with Rhodian accents. After two or three minutes, she stopped, smiled, looked at her boss, and gave him a thumbs-up.

"Are you willing to take an Arabic exam?" Praig asked.

I had just retested in Arabic and my scores showed that I was still completely conversant in the language; that was enough for Praig.

"Okay, I'm going to have to convince some of the Ops people that sending an analyst is the smart thing to do. But, believe me, it's a lot easier and a lot cheaper for me to train a linguist in operations than it is to take an operations guy and make him fluent in Greek and Arabic."

Praig managed to sell me to the skeptics in Operations based mainly on my language skills, but there was a lot more I needed to bring to the table. One essential was a deep understanding of contemporary Greek politics. After my transfer to the Directorate of Operations in April 1998, I began to "read in" to all things Greek—that is, read and digest all the available files in the agency's archives on a country where I'd be spending time on special assignment.

Terrorism was a fact of life in Greece, dating back to the 1960s, when the military, led by a group of colonels, hijacked the national government and imposed a junta that lasted seven violent and repressive years, until 1974. Once, reading a file in the Counterterrorist Center, I responded to one awful episode with a reflexive "Oh, my God."

"Are you reading the Greece files?" The question came from an adjacent cubicle.

"Yeah," I said.

"That's what everyone says when they read the Greece files," he said. Some of the episodes in the Greece files had been reported in the national and international media. And luckily, I was getting some informal help from one of the legends in the CIA's clandestine service. Gust Avrakotos had worked in Greece during the 1960s and beyond and probably knew as much about terrorism in the country as anyone around. His biggest coup, however, wasn't in Greece; it was in Afghanistan. After the Soviet Union invaded in 1979, Gust was one of the CIA's principal officers responsible for getting weapons to the mujahideen resistance, including shoulder-held Stinger missiles. Stung Soviet helicopters fell from the skies, Afghan fighters sliced and diced Soviet ground troops, and a defeated Soviet army marched out of the country a decade later, certainly one of the final nails in the coffin of the Evil Empire. Gust's exploits were featured in a book, *Charlie Wilson's War*, by the late George Crile, which focused on the efforts of the Texas congressman in the title to trump the godless Commies in Afghanistan. Both men grew thirty feet tall when they were played in the 2007 movie starring Tom Hanks as Wilson and Philip Seymour Hoffman as Gust.

By the time I met him in the late 1990s, Gust was a so-called Greenbadger—a retired officer still working for the agency under contract. He worked with me in the Counterterrorist Center as I began reading the Greece files, to which he had made many contributions, and his detailed, intimate knowledge of the country's terrorist groups helped inform my thinking. Once I was actually on assignment in Greece, we kept in regular touch; even years removed, Gust provided valuable insights, guidance, and even the names of people worth contacting. He was an abrasive guy, who could swear with the best of them and who had a difficult personal life. He had grown up in Aliquippa, a tough steel town only thirty miles from my home in New Castle, but our connection went beyond geography and a common Greek heritage. To me, Gust was a mentor—almost a second father—who helped explain a country to which I was tied by ancestry and emotion, and which had fascinated me since long before I had opened the first agency file.

Growing up, how could I not be hooked on Greece? My immigrant grandfather and grandmother came to visit every Thursday, and our family would reciprocate at least once every weekend. My grandparents were rarely without small gifts or trinkets, sometimes books, almost always having some association with the land of their birth. I was nine or ten years old when my grandfather gave me a book on Alexander the Great—the greatest Greek of them all, the old man said. Of course, I read it from cover to cover.

This was the time of the junta, and members of the Kiriakou extended family were all over the place politically. My grandmother, who read prolifically, was quite conservative, but other relatives were evenly split between conservatives and Socialists; there was even one Communist. Then, in mid-November 1973, when I was nine years old, a group of leftists protesting the junta took over the student center at the Athens Polytechnic Institute in the central part of the city. They were unarmed and demonstrating peacefully, but the colonels were having none of it; early on the morning of November 17, they sent tanks to the campus, where they opened fire on the student center, killing several dozen and wounding as many as five hundred students.

The junta had come to power in reaction to leftist political agitation that included the Socialists, a real and active Communist movement, and a near-paralysis in government. The Greeks accepted the junta partly because the colonels had the guns and partly because the military promised, in effect, to make the trains run on time. But the heavy-handed, unnecessary use of force at the student center inspired a national outcry. By the summer of 1974, the junta had collapsed, giving way to a democracy under former premier Constantine Karamanlis, who had lived in exile in Paris for more than a decade.

Democracy has prevailed ever since, but terrorism never went away. Across Europe, most of the radical groups of the sixties, seventies, and eighties—the Red Brigades in Italy, the Baader-Meinhof Gang in Germany, Action Directe in France—had either disbanded or were brought to heel by law enforcement. The Irish Republican Army and ETA, in the Basque country between Spain and France, would survive into the nineties, only to diminish in influence at the dawn of a new millennium.

Greece was different. Maybe it's a part of ancestral DNA, something having to do with a rich heritage as the cradle of European civilization, but Greeks tend to hold grudges. Two groups, ELA (for Popular Revolutionary Struggle) and 17 November, named for the day of the 1973 assault on the student center, found fresh targets for their anger starting in the mid-1970s. Stocked with lefties who had fled or were exiled during the junta years, these violent fringe groups included among their imagined enemies the European Community (later to become the European Union), NATO, almost anything American, and almost everything capitalist. Bombs were set off, shots were fired, people were killed.

For Americans and especially for Greek Americans, it became personal on December 23, 1975. Richard Welch, the CIA's senior officer in Greece, had attended a Christmas party at the U.S. ambassador's residence. He and his wife and driver had returned to his home in northern Athens. These were the days before electronic gates, so the driver pulled up and got out to open up. Four people—three men and a woman—were parked in a car directly across the street. Two masked men emerged from the backseat, and one of them shouted as they approached Welch's vehicle: "Richard Welch, get out of the car." Welch, who spoke excellent Greek, got out of the car with his wife. Their driver, meanwhile, had run for his life. One of the men said, "Richard Welch, you have been found guilty of crimes against the Greek people and you have been sentenced to death." With that, he shot Welch three times in the chest at point-blank range with a .45-caliber semiautomatic handgun. As Welch's wife screamed, the two men returned to their car, and their driver sped off.

The CIA promised Welch's widow it would do everything it could to find his killers. Meanwhile, more bombings, attacks, and other killings of Americans took place, among them navy captain George Tsantes, a U.S. defense attaché, in 1983; navy captain William Nordeen, another U.S. defense attaché, in 1988, and air force tech sergeant Ron Stewart in 1991. Everyone had a tough time tracking down the assassins, and there was widespread speculation that local law enforcement was complicit in the killings or at least tolerant of them. What's more, the terrorists were using more than small weapons like the "Welch .45"—so memorialized because the gun that killed Welch in Athens had never been found and was used time and again in other assassinations.

How the bad guys got their bigger guns amounts to a kind of comedy of terrors. Athens has a military museum right in the center of the city, an institution with a tank outside and a collection inside that would delight even the most knowledgeable armchair general. The collection includes swords and shields, battle-axes, longbows, catapults, and more. It also features an extensive array of sophisticated modern weapons—for example, rocket launchers and rocket-propelled grenades, or RPGs. Most of this stuff was displayed on the museum's walls. There was only one problem: Apparently, it never occurred to anyone at the museum to deactivate these weapons.

So there they hung, functional weapons just waiting for ammunition, until early one morning when members of 17 November descended on the museum just as it opened, tied up the security guards, and locked the door. Then they calmly and methodically removed all the live weapons from the walls, hustled them into a truck, and left without so much as a drachma for the contribution box. Next thing anybody knew, they had invaded a military depot in Larisa, a town about 150 miles north of Athens, tied up the privates and corporals on guard duty, and stolen all the rockets and grenades in sight. Later, they also attacked a police station, tied up the cops inside, and walked away with every gun and bullet in the place. When all this work was done, they were set for a couple of decades. Access to weapons would not be a problem for 17 November.

All of this information was in the public record. The Greece files at the CIA contained much more detail, based on the work of clandestine operatives and agency analysts, including the use of Athens as a kind of branch office for certain Muslim and Arab terrorist groups. But those details cannot be revealed here. Bottom line: Greece was not a patty-cake assignment, not by a long shot.

ON SEPTEMBER 1, 1998, I began the operations course at CIA training facilities in the mid-Atlantic states, including one facility widely known in press accounts as the Farm. Actually, I had been to this facility several times before for course work in writing analytical papers and learning leadership techniques. This time, I was there for weapons training, lessons in counterterrorist driving, a special operations course, and more, including instruction in a set of skills America's enemies employed far too often—the fine art of acquiring and running foreign agents to work for your country or cause.

The first day of weapons training was certainly an enlightening experience for me. I was in a group of twenty or twenty-five people, most of them ex-military, several from Special Forces units. Still, the head instructor was taking no chances. He asked two questions:

"Anybody here not own a gun? Raise your hand." My hand was the only one airborne.

"Anybody here not ever fire a weapon?" Again, one raised hand was conspicuously alone.

"Oh, Jesus, okay, we're going to start at the beginning."

Members in our group were trained in three weapons—two pistols and a shotgun. It turned out I tested at the top of the class with 100 percent on all three weapons. That was in marksmanship. But I also topped the class in the shooting gallery. This is the drill sometimes featured on television adventure shows and in the movies, where the shooter moves through a maze of fake buildings, and lifelike images of people pop up in a window or a doorway or around a corner—a woman holding a baby, for example—and the trainee has a split second to decide whether to fire.

The special operations course taught skills that might have been second nature to guys who had hunted and fished and camped in their pre-CIA days. But I was a bookish type with a fondness for big cities, decent restaurants, and comfortable beds. I wasn't accustomed to jumping out of a plane, parachuting to the ground, and living off the land for two or three days.

My orders in one particular exercise were to catch, kill, and skin a rabbit, then manage on its cooked remains. Okay, I thought at the time, I can do this, but what's the point? There can't be a lot of demand for these talents in Athens or any of the other places in southern and eastern Europe where I was likely to work on special assignments. Similarly, the part about swimming through a snake- and leech-filled swamp: I wasn't headed for the jungles of Southeast Asia, after all. I would emerge from a swamp, filthy and praying aloud for a hot shower, while most of my classmates seemed to enjoy this humbling experience. Still, I did well in this phase of training, just as I had with firearms.

The world of weapons and special operations wasn't something I had considered very seriously when I applied for transfer from the Directorate of Intelligence. No one deceived me or downplayed the abundant differences between a desk job at Langley as an analyst and fieldwork as a covert operator abroad. But the clandestine service was something of an abstract concept. I wanted this assignment because the political dynamics in the region seemed challenging. And, yes, I figured it was a way to satisfy my craving for adventure. That Greece, the land of my and my wife's heritage, was included in the package made it especially appealing. Who knows, it might even strengthen my marriage. A couple of years of this special-assignment work would do nicely, I thought, and make me an even better analyst when I returned to headquarters.

So I was taken by surprise when I not only excelled at the weaponry, the counterterrorist driving, and the other flashy stuff, but also kind of got into it, if not life in the swamps. The process of self-discovery never ceases to astonish.

THE GUNS, hand-to-hand combat, and other physical and survival training tend to dominate depictions of this training program in press accounts, popular fiction, and even nonfiction books. By comparison, tradecraft—the techniques necessary to effectively serve as a clandestine operative—gets short shrift. But inadequate tradecraft skills can be every bit as costly in blood and treasure as the misuse or abuse of automatic weapons, which is why agency instructors forced me and other trainees to practice the best methods over and over and over again.

A case officer's success abroad depends upon his or her talent for recruiting agents. Officers must improvise, but they do so at their peril if they ignore the fundamental lessons taught at the so-called Farm. Chief among them is an asset-recruitment cycle of four steps: spot, assess, develop, and recruit. The best officers are always looking for someone who has access to information of interest and use to the U.S. government. Once the officer spots such a person, whether it's at a cocktail party or a conference or a local gym, an assessment begins. What vulnerabilities does this person have? Does the person seem well disposed toward the United States? Does the person seem reliable? If the assessment suggests further movement, the officer initiates the development phase, establishing direct contact with the target and the start of a personal relationship. In the best of worlds, the relationship becomes a real, if not completely genuine, friendship. The case officer's spouse may even become friendly with the target's spouse as development unfolds. Finally, the case officer makes the pitch—the offer to work on behalf of the United States. If accepted, the target is recruited and enters the equivalent of a formal agreement, sometimes even including paperwork, with the U.S. government.

As a general rule, it is probably unwise for a case officer to pitch a target if he or she isn't nearly 100 percent certain the target will accept the offer. The chances of blowback if a target declines an offer are considerable. If the target is a citizen of the host government, for example, he or she could report the contact and the case officer could be expelled or even hurt or killed.

After a few months of practice, we could almost do these drills in our sleep. We also spent many hours on agent-pickup routines. Among the most common: The agent waits in a doorway, between buildings or near but not on a corner; the case officer drives up, pauses only as long as it takes for the agent to get in the car, then drives off.

Then there were the hundreds of hours spent practicing surveillance detection routes (SDRs), the elaborate driving routines before and after any operational act to determine whether a case officer was "red" or "black"—that is, under surveillance or free of it. The more sophisticated the trainees' SDRs were, the more their instructors liked what they saw. It wasn't a flair for intricacy or the dramatic that appealed to these experts; it was a demonstrated seriousness of purpose. On final-exam day in SDR training, one of the guys in my group never saw the five different surveillance cars on him. He had excelled at every other part of tradecraft training, but dragging surveillance to his final meeting with an agent was a sin cardinal enough to wash him out. By then, everyone knew that an error like that could cause the arrest or even the execution of an agent—someone who was already risking his life for the United States.

5

□ □ □

THE CENTRAL INTELLIGENCE Agency prides itself on training its people and preparing them for all sorts of contingencies, whether an employee works at headquarters as an analyst or works abroad as an undercover operative. In some situations I can discuss and others I cannot, that training and preparation paid off handsomely, but not without exacting a certain price.

On January 6, 1999, almost nine years to the day after setting foot in CIA headquarters as an employee, I arrived in Athens with JoAnne and our two young sons, Chris and Constantine—Costa for short. Even though I was on a temporary assignment, I'd been told I could send the family along and even rent a house on a month-to-month basis, providing I could find one. I did.

Athens was special: It was an ancestral magnet, tugging at my heart and soul, sometimes in ways that were barely comprehensible to me. It was a city of splendor and intrigue. And no small thing in my pantheon of interests, it had one of the greatest boneyards in the world.

Let me explain. When I was ten years old, I read an article in the *Pittsburgh Post-Gazette* that said a member of the Pittsburgh Pirates 1927 team was buried in New Castle, my hometown. As any baseball junkie knows, 1927 was a memorable year. The Pirates won the National League pennant, only to lose four straight to the larger-than-life New York Yankees in the World Series. It was also the year Babe Ruth hit sixty home runs during the regular season, a record that stood for thirty-four years. The cemetery was only a half mile from our house. The idea of fame in this forbidding place grabbed my attention; I had to see exactly where this guy was buried. His grave, it turned out, was unremarkable—a normal headstone with a typical inscription. But the cemetery! The cemetery was like nothing I had ever seen. New Castle in the early twentieth century was a major tin- and steel-manufacturing town, and the barons and their families had built magnificent mausoleums to house their remains in this peaceful precinct of a bustling community. The stained glass, the architecture, all of it was pure beauty to my untutored eyes. I had discovered the man-made grandeur of death, yoked to the history of our country, and I was enthralled. I needed to know and see more.

My meanderings through cemeteries over the years turned obsessive, or certainly seemed so to my friends. In college, I spent hours and hours at Arlington National Cemetery, where military men and women, presidents and paupers, are buried. Abner Doubleday, the widely acknowledged inventor of baseball, is at Arlington. So is former heavyweight champ Joe Louis, but not without the intervention of President Ronald Reagan, who waived eligibility rules prohibiting the champ's burial. I twice traveled to Richmond, Virginia, during college to visit the Hollywood Cemetery there. Jefferson Davis, president of the Confederacy, and Jeb Stuart, one of his generals. U.S. presidents James Monroe and John Tyler. Founding Father John Randolph. They all came alive, in a sense, when I came face-to-face with their mortality.

After college and graduate school, it wasn't as easy to steal away for an afternoon or a day at the cemetery. But I managed, inconveniencing myself and those close to me along the way. In South America for our honeymoon, I dragged my second wife to Eva Perón's grave in Buenos Aires, where we spent the better part of the day. Katherine has a huge heart, big enough to smile indulgently when I once drove two hours out of our way on a California trip to find an isolated village about fifty miles from Santa Barbara, where Edie Sedgwick, one of Andy Warhol's hangers-on during the 1960s, was buried after a fatal drug overdose.

CIA assignments overseas allowed me to satisfy my own peculiar addiction in more exotic locales—and none was as heady as the First Cemetery of Athens. It's a fantastical place, an urban island of life and death encircled by twelve-foot walls that embrace the late greats of Greek politics, society, science, and culture. The well-tended grounds and gardens of the Athens First offered moments of solace and respite amid all the chaos.

I was particularly interested in the grave of Alekos Panagoulis, who, as a college student, tried to assassinate one of the colonels while the junta was still in power in the early seventies. He was arrested, tortured, tried, and sentenced to death. But the junta collapsed before the sentence was carried out, and Panagoulis was released to become an instant national hero. He was elected to Parliament as a member of the PASOK, the Socialist party, and wound up in Athens's cemetery of the stars after he died in 1976 in a traffic accident. But here's the thing: Even though he hit an oil slick and collided with a taxi, resulting in his fatal injuries, the rumor was that the CIA had somehow assassinated him. How? No one could quite figure that out. But to this day, there are people on the left in Greece who believe the agency killed him.

MY BOSS IN Athens, Burt Hopper, was a terrific guy who would wind up bailing me out of major-league trouble during my final days in the Greek capital. When I got to the office that first day in town, wearing my best suit, I introduced myself around, expecting to have at least a few hours to settle in and learn where the coffeepot and men's room were. It wasn't to be. "Don't get too comfortable," Burt said. "We got a guy downstairs you need to see. He only speaks Arabic. No English, no Greek."

I was in Athens on special assignment principally to work against Greek terrorists who continued to harass and target U.S. interests. But beyond the Greek terrorists, the city also seemed populated by all sorts of groups and people who didn't exactly hold the United States, NATO, or Greece, for that matter, in very high regard. All of America's antagonists from the Middle East and North Africa were amply represented, as were most of the terrorist groups these states supported either directly or indirectly. Making matters worse, there was a widespread sense that local law enforcement turned a blind eye to the activities of foreign-born terrorists or at least put up with them so long as they didn't kill Greeks. That single proscription wasn't much of an impediment, since the Arab and Muslim terrorists were in Greece mainly because of its friendly relations with the United States and other members of the Western alliance. Greece was an American ally and a member of NATO. For the bad guys, it was a target-rich environment.

The guy downstairs underscored the point. He was a volunteer, who represented himself as an agent of a big-time terrorist group sent to Athens to do harm to the United States and its friends. His story was that he'd had a change of heart, that he had become something of a believer in truth, justice, and the American way, and that he now wanted to tell the Americans all about it. As I learned later, this wasn't all that uncommon, either in Athens or elsewhere around the world. The bad guys would send someone to a U.S. government office as a probe, hoping the Americans would bring him in for interviews and interrogation. That way, he could try to puzzle out where the office's security and defenses were positioned. That was information that might prove useful at a later date, if his masters decided to launch an attack.

I wasn't about to play it that way; instead, I told the volunteer to walk out and that he'd be picked up on a certain street corner at a specified time—in this case, at 5 a.m., before first light. If he wasn't there, I added, he needn't show up the next morning because the Americans wouldn't. But he did show at five o'clock sharp. I was in the backseat, joined by two others up front—a driver and a more senior officer—and we drove around for ten minutes, just to see if the volunteer would stick it out. This guy hung in there, which told us that his eagerness to talk was either a ruse or shoddy tradecraft.

The home team worked him for three straight days. We would pick him up on a different street corner and at a different time, then drive to an out-of-the-way location—a park on the outskirts of town, for instance, or an abandoned construction site. The idea was to make everyone comfortable so talk would come easily. The guy's story line changed each day. First, he was sent to Athens to connect with locals, make bombs, and attack the U.S. Embassy. Then it wasn't about bombs at all; he was there to track the movements of certain members of the diplomatic corps—from America and several EU countries— and pass along the information to others in his terrorist cell. And finally he claimed to have information of such value that he couldn't pass it along to mere underlings; he wanted to be escorted to the United States, where he would talk to top people in the American intelligence establishment, perhaps even DCI George Tenet himself.

Nothing added up, I thought. He said he was from country X, but his Arabic accent suggested country Y or Z. There was always another car nearby when we picked him up, and it always seemed to be somewhere in our wake. His vacant expression and slight smile when we talked among ourselves in English seemed too practiced. On the other hand, the half grin might have been a response to the fake mustache I'd pasted on for the occasion, a disguise that kept slipping on one side. We knew we had reached a point of diminishing returns. On the third afternoon, in a distant, deserted park, the senior officer turned a few degrees and reached as if to scratch his lower back; his hand returned front and center with a gun in it, quickly pointed at our Arabic-speaking friend's nose. "We're tired of playing games with you," he said in English. "What do you want with us?"

I started to translate into Arabic but was interrupted by our guest: "I guess this is the end of our relationship," he said in perfect

English. What he wanted, he confessed in language everyone understood, was the Americans' acceptance of him as a defector from radical Islam and our forbearance while he ingratiated himself by giving us information on his own government. In fact, with the gun pointed at his face, he acknowledged that he'd been sent our way as a potential double agent to spy for his masters.

We left him there on the park bench. I was a bit stunned, not because of the episode itself, but because of the way it had ended. The rules are that CIA case officers are not supposed to draw their weapons except under specific circumstances that cannot be detailed here. But it's safe to say that pulling a gun on an unarmed spy wannabe is not on the list. Besides, anytime an officer draws a weapon, permissible or not, the paperwork involved is enormous. When the team got back to the office, the senior officer addressed the problem.

"Ah, you probably don't want to write that up in the cable," he said to me, referring to our report on the affair to Langley.

Right, no way, I managed to stammer back. Not writing it up was a breach of the rules. Still, this was a man I deeply respected, and his infraction, it seemed, was pretty minor. But the drawn weapon, coming as it did on my third day on the job, had a significant impact on me—a symbol in my mind of the potential dangers in this new assignment.

IN SHORT, I was on edge from day one. I knew Americans were potential targets for Greek assassins, Arab terrorists, or just some idiot with a grudge or an urge to make a buck without working for it.

My wife JoAnne and I learned that lesson together one sunny Sunday afternoon not long after we had arrived in Greece. We'd been living in an apartment because a house was not immediately available for short-term rental. Now we were ready to move to new digs. We piled as much as we could into two cars—an older vehicle driven by JoAnne, who had the kids with her, and the brand-new BMW 540 that I just got. The Beemer was bulging, with a couple of suitcases and a giant flat-screen TV filling the backseat and visible to anyone paying attention. Our plan was to convoy to the new house. As I turned into Kifissias Boulevard, a major road in Athens, I noticed a motorcycle moving in and out of my blind spot on the right side. Every time I turned my head to look, the bike backed off, only to accelerate when my eyes returned to the traffic ahead.

My cell rang and JoAnne asked, "Do you see that motorcycle on you?" She was getting as twitchy as I was about the risks to Americans in Athens, especially a CIA operative and his family.

"Yeah, I can't shake him," I replied. "Look, why don't you drop back and let me try to get rid of him? I don't know who this guy is." I worried that it was some sort of preattack surveillance and that an assault against me or JoAnne and the kids or all of us could come around the next corner or just down the road. How long had he been on our trail? Ever since we left the apartment? *Oh, my God, this is how they do it. They're going to nail me.*

I slowed down, then sped up; he slowed down, then sped up. JoAnne had calmly made a U-turn and headed back into town. I was in the northern suburbs by now, with the traffic thinning as I vainly tried to shake this headache. When I couldn't, I tried to hit the motorcyclist, slamming on the brakes and swerving the big BMW to the right. But the guy had terrific reflexes and managed to slow down every time I went for him. By now, we were attracting the attention of other drivers, who could do nothing except keep out of our erratic flight path.

Somewhere along the way, I had unzipped the fanny pack where I'd put my gun for what I had expected to be a leisurely drive to our rented house. I could grab the gun quickly if I needed it. Finally, I hit a stoplight. I was in the far left lane; there were cars in front of me, cars behind me, cars to the right of me, and traffic to my left, moving in the opposite direction. I was completely boxed in. The motorcycle pulled up between the BMW and the car in front of me; the driver got off the bike and began moving toward my side of the BMW as he shouted in Greek, "Get out of the car! Get out of the car!"

"No," I shouted back as my hand went to the fanny pack. I grabbed the gun, lowered my window with the other, and trained the weapon on my antagonist. Big deal: The guy looked at my gun and laughed. Laughed! "I'm not afraid of you," he said. Then, he reached back into his waistband, pulled out his own gun, and began to raise it to eye level.

Case officers in training are taught to fight or flee: Make a choice and go for it. But flight is the preferred option if the odds favor an officer's escape. My car was still in drive and the light had turned green; the cars in front of me were beginning to move off. I stepped on the gas as hard I could, hitting the motorcycle and cartwheeling it along the road, and pulled away into the moving traffic before banking right and turning onto another street. I arrived at our lovely temporary house about fifteen minutes later, as shaken as I'd ever been in my life.

JoAnne had already called for help. Before the day was out, we both made sworn statements to my superiors and to the local cops. The motorcycle driver was roughly thirty years old and had a beard and a mustache, dark brown hair, an olive complexion, and a medium build. Right. This was Greece and the authorities could arrest maybe two million young men based on that description. Nobody ever found the guy and the motorcycle; they simply vanished. Sometime later, a witness to part of this little drama reported the license plate of the bike; the plate turned out to be stolen. In the end, everyone concluded that it must have been an attempted carjacking. Here was this fancy new BMW, worth more than five times an average Greek's annual income, and it's jammed with electronics to boot. I was nothing more or less than a convenient target of opportunity.

In the end, no harm, no foul. Well, not exactly. All through training, I was taught to expect the worst—especially, everyone said, in this particular national capital. Now, I'd had a taste of what could come at any moment of the day or night. It was a defining event for me. Henry Kissinger once said that even a paranoid has some real enemies. From that day forward, I always felt only a couple yards short of paranoia's fault line; every day, in my mind, the bad guys were out to get me, and they would, if I wasn't as careful as I could possibly be.

I got into six car accidents during my assignments in Greece, all of them my fault; I was so worried about surveillance that I was constantly scanning my side- and rearview mirrors and not paying attention to what was in front of me. I was forever rear-ending cars; it got to the point where I didn't even bother reporting the accidents to the insurance people. I just got out, gave the aggrieved driver my card, and said I'd be happy to pay for the repairs out of my own pocket. Unfailingly, the Greeks were delighted to oblige.

AS I MENTIONED earlier, the value of a clandestine operative's currency rises and falls with his or her relative success in recruiting and running agents—that is, people who are paid by America to deliver information considered important, directly or indirectly, to U.S. national security. I did pretty well while I was in Greece, recruiting several agents, including a man from a well-known Middle Eastern group who admitted carrying out an anti-American terrorist attack in Athens. Was there a risk of signing up a double agent? Sure. But case officers usually had their agents polygraphed, vetted them as best they could, and watched them to ensure they were playing it straight.

It obviously helped that I spoke fluent Arabic, and it was useful that my style was to avoid threats and especially violent confrontation when I pitched a potential agent. A cold pitch is hard enough when a case officer is meeting a target for the first time. I thought the best cold pitch needed to be smart and soft. There was one occasion, for example, when I learned from one of our agents that a new intelligence chief from a Mideast country was coming to town. "I think he's not a big fan of [his country's leader]," the agent said. "I think he may be somebody you can work with." Meanwhile, we were getting information from elsewhere in the U.S. intelligence community that the new intel guy was actually a big supporter of his country's leader—in fact, a true believer. Despite the disagreement, we quickly learned that there was no question about the quality of his tradecraft.

His cover was diplomatic, a commercial officer for his country. Early on, he had recruited an American teaching in Athens. One day, the teacher volunteered that he knew the military officer who had just been named the new head of a U.S. military group in Greece. In advance of his formal move, the U.S. officer would be visiting Athens to familiarize himself with the setup and meet members of the military community. The professor wanted to throw a party for him. Would his Arab friend come and meet the American colonel? The Mideast intelligence chief arrived and fell all over the new attaché: *Our people—your people and mine—have grown apart over the years. Such a shame. Perhaps we can be friends again. Let me give you something as a token of my goodwill.*

The token, which the colonel accepted a couple of days later, was an expensive carpet—a serious gift in the Middle East. I was listening to our agent explain all this and couldn't help myself: "Get out of here. No American military officer in the world would take a gift from a diplomat from [that country]." Over the years, there had been a fair amount of tension between Washington and this particular country, enough so that an exchange of gifts even in seemingly benign circumstances would have been a serious breach of security.

"No, no, I'm serious," the agent said. "I heard him [the intel chief] boasting about it."

I asked again, and the agent insisted the story was true. If so, it meant that an American defense attaché was in moral debt to a potentially hostile adversary, a compromising position indeed. This was explosive stuff.

The next morning, I went to Burt, my boss, and asked him what we should do. Burt didn't hesitate: We had to report it, but in an eyes-only cable for the DDO—the deputy director for operations. I wrote it up, had Burt vet it and sign off, then sent it to headquarters. Langley called Pentagon security officials, and they called the colonel on the carpet. He acknowledged his mistake and, as we heard later, told his Pentagon betters, "I guess I'm not going to Athens now." Or anywhere else, it turned out. They asked for and got his resignation from the military. Because of one huge lapse of judgment, he went from a full colonel with a shot at a general's star to an early pension and a blemish in his file that would last a lifetime.

His misfortune, however, delivered some good news to our people: We at least knew now that the intelligence chief was a good, professional officer—talented enough to shoot down a U.S. military rising star. I gave my agent a bonus for the valuable information and began to puzzle out how we could shut down this intel chief or maybe even bring him around to our side. I cabled headquarters and requested permission to make an approach to him. Absolutely not, headquarters cabled back, stand down immediately. Burt, to his credit, was having none of it. "Screw that," he said when I told him. "I run our operations here. I decide who gets approached in this country, not headquarters. Come up with an operational plan that makes sense and I'll sign it."

I needed to be creative: Unlike the U.S. defense attaché, I wasn't likely to run into the Mideast intelligence chief at a cocktail party. Then I remembered something I'd heard from Gust Avrakotos. Gust recalled an approach he'd made to a Soviet intelligence official in an Arab country three decades earlier. With some variations, I thought, it might work here.

My agent got the intelligence chief's home address in Athens as well as the make and model of his car. I dressed like a college kid— I wasn't graying at the temples then—and filled a backpack with textbooks, notepads, pencils, and pens. When I got to the right street, I found the intel guy's car and broke off the side-view mirror with my backpack. With the mirror in hand, I knocked on his neighbor's door, excused myself, and asked the Greek woman who answered whether that—I pointed at the car—belonged to her. No, she said, it's his car, pointing to the adjacent house. That was part of my calculation: If the intel officer happened to ask her whether she'd seen anybody break a mirror off his car, she'd give me a little protective cover. *No, but the young man who did break it came here because he thought it was my car.*

Now the moment had arrived: I knocked on the Arab's door and started to speak to him in Greek after he opened up. He put up his hand and said in English, "No, no, I don't speak Greek." He used English because it's the lingua franca; he figured that the vast majority of Greeks my age spoke it.

"Oh, you speak English," I said. "Sir, I speak English. I'm so sorry. I stopped next door and the lady told me this was your car. I was walking past it, and I was not paying attention. I'm so clumsy. My bag hit your mirror and broke the mirror off the car." It wasn't exactly Oscar worthy, but what the hell, I thought, my acting wasn't half bad.

"Dammit, this will cost me [the equivalent of $150]," he said.

"I'm so sorry. I feel terrible about this. I want to pay for the repair." There was a pause that I filled: "You speak English with a slight accent. Where are you from?"

He identified his country.

"I'm from America," I said. "You know, our people used to be such good friends. Inshallah, we will be again someday, once all this unpleasantness is behind us."

He looked at me like I was nuts. *Oh, man, that last bit probably didn't ring true to him. Slow down, don't move so fast.*

"I want to pay you for the damage," I repeated. "I feel just terrible." Then I took a big step forward and asked, "May I trouble you for a glass of water?" His brow furrowed because he knew something was up. But in Arab culture, you can never deny a request for hospitality. It's just bad manners. We'd been talking through a screen door, and the intel guy must have sensed that this stranger was playing for time, perhaps trying to get him out of the living room.

"Just a minute," he said, and he left the room to get a glass of water. As he did, I let myself in. His daughter, four years old or so, was in the living room, sitting on the floor and playing with some toys. I bent down and began to talk to her in Arabic: "What's your name, how old are you, how do you like Athens?"

My reluctant host had reentered the room and, having heard me speaking Arabic to his daughter, knew without question that this encounter was no accident. I had used Arabic with the child because I wanted to get her father's attention focused on what I might have to say. He was riveted: "What exactly do you want from me?"

"Look, I'm not going to insult you," I said. "I'm from the CIA in Washington. We've heard some nice things about you. We believe we can work with you. The bottom line is, we're the good guys. Your leader's the bad guy, and someone's bound to take him down. This is your opportunity to be on the side of the good guys." He said nothing, so I pulled out a business card, one with my real name on it, and gave it to him. "This is to prove my bona fides," I said. "It's my true name. Call this number tomorrow, ask for John Kiriakou, and I'll answer the phone. I'll be happy to meet you anywhere you want, in Greece or another country."

He put the card down on the table. "I admire your courage in approaching me," he said. "But I'm offended that you would do it in my own home."

I apologized and reiterated my interest in hearing from him.

"You have a good day," he said, showing his unwelcome visitor the door.

"You have a good day, too, sir," I said, and left.

The next day, I waited for the phone to ring, but the only call was from the agent I was running, asking for an emergency meeting. We met at 2 a.m. at an amusement park south of the city.

"Did you approach him?" the agent asked.

"Yes. What's going on?"

"He's hunkered down. He was behind a locked door all day."

"That's good," I said. "He's not going to report the approach to his bosses because, if he does, they're going to call him back and they may very well execute him. And he knows it."

"Well, I don't know what's happening, but he's panic-stricken," my agent said. "There's no way he's going to say anything to the folks back home. You scared the hell out of him."

Sure enough, no one said a word. Three years later, the intel guy called my old number and got another CIA officer doing temporary duty in Athens; he knew the whole story of my approach. "I need to talk to John Kiriakou," the Mideast officer said. Now, when it was long past too late, he wanted to talk. But the case officer in Athens asked him for something—something sensitive—to test his willingness to help.

"I am a patriot, loyal to my country," he said. "I cannot give you such a thing." That was the end of it—and the end of agency contact with him, at least so far as I knew.

So was this pitch a failure? Yes and no. Yes, because I did not succeed in recruiting him to work for the United States. No, because the approach effectively shut down his operations in Athens. He'd been penetrated. He knew the Americans knew about him, and that constrained his freedom of movement. He couldn't raise a warning flag at home because it would risk his life to reveal that his leader's adversaries had approached him. The outcome wasn't as good as opening a pipeline of information from his country's embassy, but rendering that embassy deaf, dumb, and blind in Athens was a damn fine second prize.

6

□ □ □

GREEK TERRORISM WASN'T confined just to Greece, and that was the beauty of the job. If there was a Greek Communist in Italy I needed to talk to, I could hop a flight to Rome. If there was a connection to the network of Carlos the Jackal, the notorious terrorist arrested a few years earlier, and I needed to see somebody in Paris who could talk about it, I ran off to France. The former Soviet Union was very active in Greece in the 1970s, and I often wondered if there was a connection between the intelligence services of the former Communist countries of Eastern Europe and Greece's hard-left terrorist groups.

In 1991, not long after the collapse of the Soviet empire, a general from an eastern European country agreed to go to an FBI training program in New Orleans, Louisiana. In the bad old days of Soviet-style Communism, Radomir Zhivkov had been such a true believer in Marxist-Leninist nonsense that they used to call him Radomir the Red. But after the fall, he was able to recognize Moscow's corrupt and stultifying ideology for what it was. He was still a true believer; the difference now was that he believed in democracy, free markets, and especially the rule of law made by elected representatives, not dictators. In the postcommunist world, he was interested in making the transition from a military career to law enforcement, which was why he ended up in New Orleans.

His training evaluation at the end of the course was in his file, part of the voluminous material I had read before heading to southern and eastern Europe on temporary assignment. Radomir testified to his new faith in the institutions of the West and said he looked forward to working with the Americans in the future. But no one from any U.S. government entity contacted him afterward. He seemed to disappear from America's radar screens.

I found it stunning but not terribly surprising. One of the problems with some CIA operatives in the field is that they don't read files because they don't think like analysts. They glance quickly at the two or three cables on top of the file, then run with whatever idea they've cooked up—sometimes without thinking much about the hook to catch the fish. There was a terrific hook for Radomir, separate and apart from his apparent affection for Americans, but no one had twigged to it, which was why, I supposed, no one had followed up with him

Radomir lived on turf outside my area of temporary assignment, so I had to cable headquarters to ask whether I could approach him, assuming the Red was still around. Yes, he's around, I was told by my bosses, but we don't think there's any useful purpose in contacting him. From their point of view, I was on my own: They were fine with an approach, providing the money and any subsequent expenditures came out of my operational budget. Burt, my boss in the region, approved the trip; I flew to Radomir's country and tracked him down to a small office in what may have been a Russian Mafia bank, where he worked as head of security for about forty dollars a week. From his file, I was betting that this wasn't what Radomir had in mind when he said he wanted to work in law enforcement.

His door was open, but I knocked anyway, walked in, and wasted no time when Radomir looked up: "General Zhivkov," I said, extending my hand. "My name is John Kiriakou from the CIA in Washington, and I'm here to change your life." Really, that's exactly what I said.

Radomir blinked several times rapidly before he answered. "Please, my friend, sit down, sit down. I've waited a long time for this day."

"General, I understand that nobody knows as much about your country's intelligence service and its activities in Greece in the 1970s as you do."

"I think this is correct," Radomir said. "What is it that you want?"

What the United States wanted was anything that could shed further light on the murder of Americans by 17 November, particularly the 1975 assassination of Richard Welch, head of the CIA's office in Athens at that time. Operational details must remain off limits here, but with Radomir's invaluable help, we were able to identify the link between Ilich Ramírez Sánchez, the infamous Venezuelan-born terrorist also known as Carlos the Jackal, and 17 November. The link was a fairly prominent Greek businessman who was important in PASOK and who also had an office in Zhivkov's country. Radomir was a retired general from the days of Soviet domination, but he was not without some lingering influence in his newly democratic country. He asked his country's intelligence service to tap the Greek businessman's phone and secure all the transcripts. With that, we worked with his country in a joint operation to bring down this Greek conduit between 17 November and Carlos the Jackal, who had assisted the terrorist group in securing arms and gathering intelligence.

I visited Radomir's country a dozen times during my time in the region. He was a superb agent, who earned and kept our trust by his various good deeds. And the agency did right by him, too. He didn't want to be paid, which itself was remarkable for an agent. "I wouldn't feel comfortable taking money from you," he told me. "I'm a national patriot, and it would be wrong to take money from a foreign government."

But he clearly needed money. I knew that Radomir was fiercely proud of his grandson, who was graduating from his country's equivalent of high school and who wanted to go on with his education. "Radomir, let me do this," I said. "We'll pay for your grandson's college education anywhere he wants to go in the world. If it's an American university, we have an office that can help him arrange that, too." Radomir was thrilled. His grandson felt more comfortable staying home and going to a local university. That proved a lot easier on the agency's pocketbook, but the CIA would have gladly paid the tab had his grandson chosen Harvard or Stanford.

By this time, in the late nineties, the political climate in Greece had begun to shift. For the better part of two decades after the murder of Richard Welch, the 17 November group was widely regarded as a band of Robin Hoods, standing up for the common man and attacking bad people, or those perceived to represent bad people. Americans fell into this category and probably would have topped the imaginary enemies list if it weren't for the Turks. But 17 November targeted Greeks, too, so long as they were perceived to be tools of the military or conservative and right-wing organizations. In 1985, one victim was a newspaper publisher; in 1986 and 1988, Greek industrialists. In these murders and attempted murders, collateral damage was rare, which was one reason the mayhem did not seem to dent 17 November's reputation as a defender of the downtrodden. Most Greeks felt the group's victims deserved what they got. In fact, the group never earned that misplaced goodwill among Greece's working class by delivering social services the way, say, the Palestinian terrorist group Hamas first achieved its popularity on the West Bank and Gaza Strip. No, 17 November's work was murder in the name of a credo that no longer existed.

Turning the tide against terrorism isn't easy, but the good guys can always hope that the bad guys go too far. And for once, 17 November did. On the morning of September 26, 1989, parliamentary deputy Pavlos Bakoyannis was coming out of the elevator of his apartment building in the Kolonaki neighborhood, a beautiful and upscale area of Athens. Several 17 November killers were waiting for him; they shot him repeatedly, making sure he was dead before they fled the scene.

He was the first active politician to be murdered, and 17 November could not have chosen its target with less appreciation for public sentiment. Bakoyannis was immensely appealing, perhaps the most popular political figure in Greece. He had opposed the colonels' takeover of Greece in 1967 and even made radio broadcasts from exile attacking the junta. He was a liberal who was a leading light in the New Democracy Party and who helped engineer an alliance between conservatives and the Communist Party that eventually pushed the Socialists and Prime Minister Andreas Papandreou out of government.

Greeks across the political and social spectrum, from the monied precincts of the right to Communists and Socialists on the left, were outraged by Bakoyannis's assassination. From that day forward, 17 November's purchase on public support steadily weakened. The group continued to murder and bomb, but with the help of Radomir the Red and other informants during the 1990s, its adversaries—and America's clandestine case officers proudly counted themselves among them—were slowly closing in.

GREECE WAS NOT a regular stop on European swings by American presidents. Dwight David Eisenhower visited in December 1959, near the end of his presidency, and George H. W. Bush paid a call in July 1991. That was it, two presidents in four decades, until President Bill Clinton arrived in 1999. Despite warnings from the intelligence community, the White House was bound and determined to include Greece in a November presidential trip, especially since Clinton was also touching down in Turkey, Greece's longtime adversary. But the timing wasn't great, to put it mildly. His trip, originally planned for November 13 to 15, was trimmed back after a series of early November protests, a bomb explosion or two, and even a tableau featuring a mock trial of the president and a hanging of his effigy. The list of grievances was long, from U.S. support of the junta in the late sixties and early seventies to the recent bombing of Yugoslavia, an offense to Greece and its traditional Serbian allies. The president's visit, cut back to less than twenty-four hours, was reset for November 19 to hopscotch a critical day on every Greek's calendar.

November 17, the day the military junta bloodily crushed a student protest, the inspiration for the radical group of the same name, was a day for celebration by Greeks, not a day for Americans trying to befriend Greeks. There were always marches commemorating the day, even as 17 November's grip on the popular imagination was loosening, and there were always demonstrations in front of the U.S. Embassy and even red paintballs tossed at its façade, symbolic gestures of disdain for American backing of the junta. On November 17, 1999, more than ten thousand people filled the streets, protesting Clinton's upcoming arrival and just about everything else American.

The next evening, in the center of Athens, several banks were burning—the result of Molotov cocktails tossed by assorted anarchists, Communists, and maybe even a few 17 November types, although small firebombs normally would have been beneath their dignity as self-reverential terrorists. Friday, November 19, 1999, when Clinton arrived, central Athens seemed like a ghost town because Greek authorities had limited protests to an area several miles away from his motorcade's route. In addition to Secretary of State Madeleine Albright and National Security Adviser Sandy Berger, Hillary and Chelsea Clinton were accompanying the president, with the entire entourage staying at the Intercontinental Hotel, some distance from the U.S. Embassy. Security was tick tight.

During a presidential visit abroad, nearly every American in an official capacity gets pressed into duty, even if the stop is only for a few hours. Exceptions were not made for CIA officers on temporary assignment. My job was to take notes at Clinton's late afternoon meeting in his Intercon presidential suite with the leader of the opposition, Costas Karamanlis, nephew of former prime minister Constantine Karamanlis, who was a towering figure in twentieth-century Greek politics. Albright, Berger, and U.S. ambassador Nicholas Burns attended, of course, as did Karamanlis's foreign-affairs and military advisers. For all that intellectual firepower in the room, very little substance came out of it. This was happy talk—we love you, you love us—and why not? Greece was two decades past military dictatorship, a flourishing democracy with its share of troubles but a country now committed to peaceful transitions of power.

The Greeks left after the meeting ended. Then the president and Berger walked out, the two of them chatting, followed a half minute later by Albright and Burns. Albright was upset about something: "These Greeks, they're such horrible people," she said to the ambassador. "I don't know how you live here." What apparently bugged her was the Greek government's penchant for telling Washington what it wanted to hear, particularly about its commitment to combat terrorism, then never acting on the promise.

Berger ended his conversation with Clinton; suddenly, I found myself four feet away from the president of the United States—in effect, all dressed up and no place to go. Then the elevator door opened and Hillary and Chelsea walked out. As they approached him, the president, making small talk, said something about how much they'd all enjoyed the Parthenon that morning; the head of the Parthenon Museum had given them a personal tour at 10 a.m. Hillary did not appear happy, so the president repeated his thought: "We sure had a good time at the Parthenon this morning, didn't we, Hill?"

"Jesus Christ, Bill, it rained all day. I'll be in the room." After which she walked past him with Chelsea in tow. You had to feel for the guy. Maybe it was a lingering hangover from the Monica Lewinsky mess, but this was rough treatment, particularly in front of strangers. Clinton chewed his lip for a couple of seconds before he turned to me and said, "Let's get the hell out of here."

"Yes, sir," I said and followed him and three Secret Service agents into the elevator. We were headed to a lower level ballroom where the president had to deliver a speech on trade and business relations to an audience of 1,200 that included the Hellenic-American

Chamber of Commerce, an American women's association, and all the U.S. Embassy families. He had only three or four minutes to marshal his composure; he did that and more, delivering a terrific speech that drew several standing ovations. For the first time, I saw up close what they meant about Clinton magic before big crowds.

In fact, President Clinton did and said all the right things on the trip. He gave that great speech. He became the first American president to apologize for U.S. support of the military junta. And he left Americans in Athens with nothing but warm feelings about him.

Amazingly, his visit also had a profound impact on the Greek press. For the two weeks prior to Clinton's arrival, the printed and electronic media were on the warpath, with commentators across the political spectrum claiming the American president wasn't welcome in Greece. What really got to me and many other Americans was the way they referred to him—not as president of the United States, but as "*O Planetarhis,*" which translates as "the planet ruler." It was a phrase concocted for the moment, and if it was intended to offend Americans, and it was, the ploy was successful. Americans in Greece took pride in their country. This kind of dissing was uncalled for. The Greeks were portraying the American government and its politicians as a bunch of fascists and imperialists; at the same time, they ignored Serbian atrocities against the Muslim population in Yugoslavia.

But the trip went so smoothly and Clinton said such nice things about Greece that the press did a complete 180 after he left. Suddenly, he was "President Clinton" again. One particularly virulent critic on TV said the reporters, editors, and pundits, and he included himself, should be ashamed of themselves. The president had extolled the virtues of Greece; he could have complained about his chilly reception, compared to the idolatrous greetings he got in Sofia and Istanbul, but he didn't. And he could have complained about terrorism, but he didn't.

That he didn't was all the more remarkable because the central purpose of the trip was to broker an agreement between the two countries to join forces in the battle against terrorism. The details had been worked out and no roadblocks seemed in the way, except, apparently, for one called Greek pride. Given all the anti-American demonstrations attending Clinton's truncated trip, the Greek government clearly worried about the appearance of meek acquiescence to U.S. "demands." In the end, the Greeks took a pass on the agreement; it was never signed. No wonder Madeleine Albright was pissed off.

The world was on the lip of a new millennium; after nearly four decades of domestic terrorist acts committed by Greeks against Greeks in the name of a discredited ideology, the people were still without a government prepared to go to war against the bad guys.

But 17 November was beginning to implode, even though its members still reveled in their own mythology. In less than three years, two events—a murder and an errant bomb—would bring it low once and for all.

7

□ □ □

AS I HAVE said before, work at the CIA—whether you labor in a cubicle in Langley, Virginia, or travel the world on behalf of your country—isn't what used to be called banker's hours in the days when bankers worked from nine to five. The business of running foreign agents could be particularly unnerving. These were sensitive operations, and I couldn't exactly meet with agent-recruits during the day. Most of the time, the meetings were set for the wee hours of the morning, which meant I had to leave the house in the late evening and drive for three hours doing surveillance detection runs to make sure I wasn't being followed. After a one-hour meeting, I'd do the anti-surveillance work again. This routine left me bone tired two or three days a week and on edge every waking hour of every day.

Part of my problem was that my marriage was falling apart. JoAnne and I came from families where long marriages were the norm. Her parents and my parents had both been married about forty years, and their marriages were rock solid. The two of us? Not so much. Our marriage, as I indicated earlier, was troubled from the very start. JoAnne's behavior of choice for dealing with perceived emotional wounds continued to be the silent treatment.

My line of work certainly didn't help. She knew I worked for the CIA, and that my initial job as an analyst was thinking big thoughts about big issues and writing papers about them at headquarters in suburban Virginia. I had often left for Langley early in the morning and stayed late into the evening; she grudgingly wrote off this routine as a condition of my employment. After all, I returned home every night, just like any white-collar laborer in the many fields that serve the U.S. government in Greater Washington.

But she was plainly upset by what she sensed as a change in me during and after my training at the so-called Farm. I never went into the specifics of weapons training or tradecraft, but she maintained that something fundamental had transformed me. "You're a different person now," JoAnne said, and it wasn't meant as a compliment.

How? I really wanted to know how she perceived this new alien figure in her life. I could plead guilty to greater maturity and a strengthened confidence in my ability to handle the rigors of my chosen work. Perhaps JoAnne's emotional parsing of these traits translated as tough, callous, and unforgiving. But she was never very precise, so I was left to grope for answers to questions that hadn't been asked.

Amazingly, given the growing distance between us, my wife accepted the middle-of-the-night absences in Athens, at least at first. I couldn't talk in detail about what I was doing, just that I had appointments that were a part of my work. But after several months, she became convinced I was having an affair—and on that matter, she found her voice.

"Oh, it's business," she'd say. "What's her name?" I wasn't having an affair; I would swear to that under oath and wired up for a lie detector. But she was having none of it. After four or five months, she moved into the guest room of our temporary digs. We were barely speaking at that point.

The divorce rate in the CIA is sky-high, and part of the reason is the stress such working conditions put on marriages. But despite accumulating evidence to the contrary, I always believed my marriage was stronger than that.

I begged her to believe me, promising to do anything to prove that I was telling the truth, that I wasn't cheating on her. She was deaf to my pleas.

I had two men, both Greeks, both really good guys, who guarded our house and, in effect, watched our back. One day, Dimitri, one of the two, sidled over after I got home and pointedly commented on how good my wife was looking these days.

"Yeah? What do you mean?"

"Man, haven't you noticed? She's lost weight, she bought all new clothes, she's colored her hair. She's looking good." Dimitri clearly sensed a disturbance in the Force. The truth was, I hadn't noticed. In retrospect, it was clear she was trying to send me a signal, but I wasn't receiving.

Soon after Dimitri's remarks, my wife said she had to go on the Pill. "I'm having some female problems, and the birth-control pill will help."

"We've been married twelve years and you need to go on the Pill now?" But I thought, what the hell did I know? So I drove her to the gynecologist.

Now, my wife had inherited her late grandmother's house on the island of Chios. The house was made of fieldstone and in some disrepair; before we left for my temporary work in Greece and elsewhere in the region, JoAnne said that she wanted to fix up her grandmother's old place and take the kids there so they could get to know their cousins. It would also improve their Greek.

I thought it was a terrific idea. So JoAnne would go once a month for a couple of days. Then it was twice a month, then once a week. Then she started to take our older son out of school for a day to extend that weekly visit. Maybe the altered pattern should have raised my suspicions or triggered some sort of bullshit meter, but it didn't. I was always fighting exhaustion to stay sharp in my work, and my wife's increasingly frequent jaunts to Chios were welcome. They reduced the number of distractions.

Early on the morning of April 18, 2000, my oldest son, Chris, who was just four days shy of his seventh birthday, was sitting on the floor in the bathroom watching his old man begin to shave. Shaving around the mouth must have reminded Chris of something because he went from talking about his upcoming school day to this:

"Daddy, I told Mommy she shouldn't kiss Uncle Stelios on the lips like that. She should only kiss you on the lips like that. And she told me to mind my own business."

I wiped the shaving cream off my face very slowly, trying without much success to control my emotions, then went to the guest room and kicked the bed.

"What?" she said, coming awake.

"Who the fuck is Stelios?"

Suddenly, she was fully awake. "Where did you hear that name?"

"Who is he, JoAnne?"

"Don't believe everything a six-year-old says."

I could feel the anger building in me. Not good. "I'm going to leave," I told her, "before I do something I'll regret for the rest of my life." So half-shaven, I got dressed, grabbed my guns, got in the car, and headed for work.

About 2 p.m., the phone on my desk rang. I ignored it just as I had ignored the constant calls on my cell. I didn't want to talk to her. Finally, one of my colleagues picked up my landline.

"Buddy, your wife's on the phone and she's really upset."

"Yeah, she ought to be upset," I said, punching the flickering button on my phone.

"What?" I shouted at her.

She was in tears. "I was just in this terrible car accident. I think my wrist is broken, the kids are crying, the car's totaled." She told me where she was and that the kids seemed to be all right; I called my two security guards, filled them in, and asked them to meet me at the accident scene. The car was demolished. JoAnne was semihysterical, but she was cogent enough to tell me what had happened. She was in the left-hand lane signaling a left turn with five cars behind her. Greeks never wait in line. They'll all edge up to the front, then all try to make the left turn at the same time. That's what happened. Just as JoAnne was making her left, the guy at the end of the line passed all the cars in front of him on the left. He hit her broadside, pushing her vehicle up onto the sidewalk and into a tree. Fortunately, the air bags deployed.

The guy who caused all this mayhem walked up to me, shaking and upset.

"What the hell happened here?" I really wanted to hear how he was going to try to wriggle out of this.

"I wanted to make a left and your wife wanted to make a left and we ran into each other," he said.

"You ran into each other?" I was furious. "You were at the back of the line, she told me. You hit her when she went to make the left."

He said she was lying, I said she wasn't. We went back and forth like that a few times, and then he said to me, in Greek, "Ah, your wife, she's a whore."

I snapped. "My wife's a whore?" I screamed it back at the guy and bang! I hit him as hard as I could, right in the face. The guy was stunned. I hit him fast two more times and he went down. Then I blanked, remembering nothing until the two guys who watched my house and my back arrived on the scene and pulled me off. Later, they told me I was on top of the driver, holding his hair and beating his head against the pavement. *I could have killed him. I would have killed him, if my guardian angels hadn't gotten there first.*

"Are you insane?" Dimitri bellowed. "Are you insane?" At that blind moment, there probably was only one honest answer. I had never been in a fistfight in my entire life, not even in the schoolyard as a kid. I didn't even know how to hit someone, which was why I wrecked my hand. I'd hit the guy full fist, shattering the two weaker knuckles; it's called boxer's fracture, I learned later, just before the first of three surgeries.

By this time, traffic had come to a standstill; horns were blaring and the spectacle of a car crash, strong words, and a fight had drawn quite a crowd of onlookers. The police arrived and, after cursory explanations, took everyone involved to the local station, where the top cop asked whether I was an American official. Yes, I said.

"Okay, sit in the cell," the cop said. "We're going to call your embassy and work this out."

"I'm very sorry for what I did," I told him, probably saying more than I should have. "I lost it on the guy. He called my wife a whore and I lost it."

The police officers nodded sympathetically but didn't say much. They let me sit in an open cell while they called the embassy, and they didn't bother to take my gun, which was still in my fanny pack.

Their attitude wasn't surprising: The Greeks hate confrontation. The guy I hit was a baker, and he didn't deserve the pounding he got. After the baker was patched up at the hospital, the police brought him to the station to see if they could smooth everything over. I said I was willing to shake hands and forget it, but the baker wanted to press charges. The police captain asked the two of us to tell our stories.

I told my tale and the police captain said, "Is this true? Did you call his wife a whore?" The baker acknowledged he did. The captain said he had a beating coming to him for that insult and asked us to shake and call it a day. Again, the baker refused. I put my hand over my heart and apologized for the assault. It wasn't for show: I meant it on more levels than the baker or the police captain could possibly know. What I had done was inexcusable, a terrible breach of restraint, even given the provocation. I had made an utter fool of myself. Worse, I had put my employer—not the CIA but the U.S. government—in the crosshairs of a potentially embarrassing international incident.

"Look," the captain said to the baker, "we're going to arrest you for the accident and we're going to allow him to press charges against you for calling his wife a whore. That's defamation of character, and it's a crime in Greece."

Finally, the baker wilted, but he still refused to shake my hand. I was free to go.

But that wasn't the end of it. One of my security guards was on his cell phone in the police station's waiting room, just ringing off when I walked out.

"The ambassador wants to see you right away," he said. I must have turned ashen. *That's it, I'm finished. Good-bye, Greece. Good-bye, career. Good-bye, reputation. Good luck finding other work.*

My arrival at the embassy didn't exactly lift my spirits: "Good luck, John," someone said. There was some gallows humor—appropriate enough, I supposed, for someone being observed as a dead man walking. I headed straight for the office of Ambassador Nicholas Burns, whom I had met years earlier in Saudi Arabia. In those days, Burns had a reputation as someone who flat-out hated the CIA.

Burt, my boss, met me outside the ambassador's office and got right to the point:

"What the hell was this all about?"

"Burt, I'm ashamed of myself," I tried to explain. "It's all my fault. I'm ready to take it like a man." I had screwed up big-time, but was I now contemplating martyrdom?

"All right, all right, just try to keep quiet in there and let me do the talking," said Burt. "I've got a couple of ideas."

The ambassador was livid and, at that moment, not given to the language of diplomacy.

"What the fuck went through your head?" It was a rhetorical question, but I had already forgotten Burt's injunction and answered anyway.

"Ambassador, I'm so sorry, I can't excuse what I did," I said. "But I can explain my actions. If you're willing to listen, I'm willing to tell you."

"I don't even want to know the details," Burns said. "I don't care why you did it. The *fact* that you did it means you've got to go.

Tomorrow morning, ten o'clock on Delta." That was the next scheduled flight to New York.

It was over, but I couldn't let it go: "Okay, it's my own fault, getting expelled, but let me explain." In Burt's eyes, I was beyond help; even so, he came to the rescue.

"Wait, wait, wait one second," he said. "Ambassador, first of all, this guy deserves a good ass kicking. Second of all, the cops aren't charging him with anything. They let him go. Third, there's been no press involvement, at least not yet." I didn't know where Burt was going with this, but I finally knew enough to keep my lip buttoned.

"What I would propose is, let's wait a day," Burt said to Burns. "If this doesn't make the press, we let him stay. He's done good work here. If it does make the press, I'll drive him to the airport myself."

Burns did not appear happy with Burt's counter; he'd been boxed in and he knew it.

"Well, all right, but if it's in any of the papers," he said pointing at me, "you're out of here."

I had hand surgery that afternoon, arriving at the hospital just as JoAnne was leaving after her own surgical repairs, and got home around nine o'clock. She was shedding tears as I walked in. I told her not to waste them. "This happened because of you," I said. "I did this to protect your honor, and your honor didn't deserve to be protected." Emotionally exhausted, I headed for the bedroom and crashed.

The next morning, I shaved as best I could with my left hand, got in the car, and drove one-handed to work. Everybody wanted to hear the story, but I begged off. There was nothing I could honestly say to diminish my embarrassment at making such an undisciplined fool of myself. Besides, I was too busy praying. *Maybe Burt's gambit will work. Maybe the Greek papers haven't heard about the incident or, if they have, maybe they thought it wasn't newsworthy. Maybe I have a chance of surviving this.*

The folks in the U.S. Information Service office, who monitor the Greek press, said there were no reports of an American losing it in the middle of the previous afternoon and beating the shit out of a poor baker. Burt told his excited subordinate to calm down. "Let's wait one more day," he counseled. "If there's nothing, we'll take the ambassador's temperature and see where we go from there. Maybe it'll blow over." And it did: The papers never did run a story, and the ambassador gave me a stay of execution. I'd earned a reputation as something of a nut, but the diplomatic imbroglio everyone anticipated hadn't happened. I was free to return to my duties—a case officer on temporary assignment in Greece and other ports of call in southern and eastern Europe.

My domestic situation needed attention. JoAnne had always vehemently denied being involved with anyone else and said marriage counseling was unnecessary. Although she finally agreed to give it a try, it was a joke almost from the very beginning. She got stuck in traffic going to the first appointment—with an Anglican priest who'd agreed to talk to us—and eventually turned around and went home rather than show up late. A guy at the U.S. Embassy who ran some sort of religious study group said he'd give it a try. At the first session, she wouldn't speak—nothing in response to his invitation to talk about her view of our marriage. Then, at his suggestion, I left the room and they talked for forty-five minutes. But she wouldn't tell me what they had discussed.

At the second session, our counselor suggested a half hour with each of us privately in an adjoining room. I went first, laying out my view of what had gone wrong—the absence of communication, the silences, her suspicions, and, of course, my belief that she had betrayed our marriage vows. Then it was JoAnne's turn; after a half hour, the door opened and she walked right by me without even making eye contact; as I learned later, she left the embassy and drove home.

"What gives?" I knew the answer but had to ask him anyway.

"Look, I'm sorry, but she doesn't want to be married to you anymore," he said.

"What the hell's that supposed to mean?"

"She's unwilling to try to work this out," the counselor said, repeating what he'd said about her not wanting to be married to me. "I'm sorry. I can't help you."

That was in mid-May 2000. Within three months, the two of us separated and she and the boys left for New York.

IN EARLY 2000, Stephen Saunders arrived in Athens as the new defense attaché at the British Embassy. Stephen was an engaging guy, popular within the diplomatic community and among Western military and intelligence figures. One night at a party, we got to talking about security precautions; Saunders was gently needling me about my car, the BMW 540, which was fully armored, and about the two handguns I always carried. And the body armor the Brits' American cousins sometimes wore. "You Americans, you're so obsessed with security," Saunders said. "Nothing's going to happen to you here. This is Greece! This is an EU country. This is a NATO country."

Saunders was a fifty-three-year-old brigadier, the equivalent of an American one-star general, a worldly man who should have had a keen appreciation of the risks to Brits and Americans in Greece. Maybe he was joking, but I didn't think so at the time. "You guys, you live in a dream world," I told him. "If you think just because it's EU and NATO and pretty here that they're not going to kill you, you're crazier than I am." We laughed and turned to another subject.

A few weeks later, having returned to Athens from an assignment elsewhere in the region, I was driving down Kifissias Avenue, a straight, ten-mile shot down the hillside from my house to my office. Traffic was always heavy, but on this day, it seemed as bad as anything I'd seen. The radio station was reporting a traffic incident of some sort and urging drivers to take alternative routes. But any alternative would have required a huge detour, so I kept moving forward as best I could. The next radio report described the scene ahead as a "criminal incident" that had closed two of the three lanes on my side of the road. As I inched along, wondering what was happening ahead, I finally spotted a car in one of the closed lanes. A bit further and the scene resembled a war zone, with shattered glass everywhere and blood all over the interior of the car. *Oh my God, somebody was killed. This has got to be a terrorist attack. Those bastards hit someone again.*

It was too risky for official Americans and "guests" from a few other countries to have diplomatic plates, so the Greeks in their infinite wisdom had assigned three letters—YHB for Americans—followed by a number. My plate was YHB1442. The British were YBH and a number. As I drew closer, I could see the plate was YBH. For a moment, though, I forgot that the letters designated a British car; instead, I assumed a terrorist saw the transposed letters, mistakenly thought it was an American, and popped some innocent Greek instead of his imagined target. A second later, it dawned on me that it was a British car, a white Rover, and that it belonged to Stephen Saunders.

Saunders had been driving to work alone on Kifissias Avenue at eight in the morning when two masked gunmen on a motorcycle opened fire after Stephen stopped in heavy traffic. One of the weapons of choice was a .45 pistol, *the* Welch .45, and the gunmen got away by snaking their motorcycle through traffic. Saunders died at a nearby hospital later that morning. A few weeks passed before 17 November claimed responsibility for the assassination—payback, the group said in a letter to a newspaper, for Saunders's work helping to coordinate the NATO bombing of Serbia the previous year.

Saunders's wife, Heather, was quite a woman, somehow managing to maintain her composure throughout the ordeal. She did more than that: She also appeared on Greek television and said all the right things—that the killing of her husband was a crime against the Greek people and against all of Greek society, and that only barbarians act with such callous disregard for human life.

The murder of the parliamentary deputy Pavlos Bakoyannis more than a decade earlier had begun to raise questions about 17 November in the minds of many Greeks. Even so, the killings had continued, and nothing much had been done by Greek law enforcement to stop them. Now, the death of Stephen Saunders, followed by a campaign launched by his widow against the terrorist group that killed him, was finally reshaping public opinion for good. Greece had been picked to host the summer Olympics of 2004, and worries about the country's public image were spreading. Popular revulsion against 17 November combined with increased official pressure to shut down the group's activities. The Saunders hit was its last.

Two years later, the police got lucky when a bomb held by 17 November member Savvas Xeros accidentally exploded, seriously injuring him. Xeros had names, plenty of names, and a safe house. Thinking he was going to die, Xeros confessed to everything. Before long, the police had a long list of 17 November suspects. In December 2003, a Greek court handed down a guilty verdict against fifteen members of the group for crimes stretching back to the mid-1970s. The group's leader, Alexandros Yiotopoulos, and its leading hit man, Dimitris Koufodinas, called "Poison Hand," allegedly because everything he touched died, were each convicted on 956 separate counts; they both received sentences of life without parole.

NICK BURNS, THE ambassador, had no reason to end my temporary assignment and ship me home when the Greek press, either through ignorance or benign neglect, hadn't reported my street brawl. But my time in the region was drawing to an end. After the Saunders assassination, everyone waited for the inevitable communiqué from 17 November, which always delivered a long diatribe, sometimes twenty-five or thirty pages long, listing the usual Marxist-Leninist claptrap that supposedly led to its decision to kill. Think of "Unabomber" Ted Kaczynski's 1995 manifesto, all thirty-five thousand words of it, and you'd get some idea of the tone and substance of these 17 November jeremiads.

The group stayed true to form and took its grievances public in early August 2000. It was the usual stuff, except for a passage that snapped my head back and caught the attention of my bosses. Finally getting to the killing itself, the communiqué said in part: "We saw the big spy, but he was in an armored car and we knew that he was armed. So we elected to carry out the sentence on the war criminal Saunders." *I had always been so careful. I never took the same route two days in a row. I always left the office at a different time, always reported suspicious vehicles. How the hell did they find me?*

Burt made it plain that I had no choice: He expected me to clear out of Dodge as quickly as I could. The bad guys knew who I was. They knew where I lived, which was only two blocks from Saunders. They knew the particulars of my automobile. They knew I carried guns at all times. Burt complimented me on my work during this assignment. I had recruited five people in eighteen months, including Arabs; that compared with Burt's own record of nine recruits in twenty-five years abroad. "But it's over for you here," my boss told me. "They know too much about you. You've got to go." I was on a flight to New York the next day.

I was entitled to five weeks of home leave—a good time, I figured, to see whether the private sector could use someone with my particular skills at risk analysis and to file for divorce now that JoAnne and I were formally separated. Using my brother's New York apartment as a base, I interviewed with a bunch of banks and investment houses and found some interest, including one offer with a caveat: We're about to be acquired, the word was, and there's a high risk of major layoffs once the deal is closed. With two young kids and child-support payments, it seemed pointless: I thanked them for their honesty and moved on.

In late September, having been assigned to a branch of the CIA that was training officials and military officers of certain foreign countries in counterterror operations, I reported to my new boss at headquarters. He obviously knew what had happened in Athens, and he was sympathetic. He and others said I had made some enemies at Langley, chief among them the director of European operations, one Mary Margaret Graham. She thought I used a heavy hand in my work, or so went the story, citing my brash recruitment of an eastern European general, the business of breaking off a side-view mirror, and, of course, the cherry-red frosting I had detailed on an Athens baker's face. My new boss told me that I'd have to sit in the penalty box for a year or so. "Keep your head down, do your job, and don't fuck up," he said. "Don't beat anybody up. And you're going to be okay." The advice was much appreciated. I intended to do exactly what he suggested.

A short time later, I got an e-mail from the American who took my temporary house after JoAnne and I left. The guy wanted to know whether I had ever noticed a red Toyota watching the house. I had seen a black Citroën and reported it to U.S. security officers, who could always check the license plates; it turned out the Citroën's owner had some houses in the area and was just checking on his properties.

"Well, I've got a red Toyota on my house and the license plates are stolen." His bosses weren't taking any chances: The guy decamped and shipped out of Athens.

Not long after my evacuation, I was developing some film I had shot when my parents visited Athens in late June 2000, just a few weeks before my departure. One picture stood out from the rest, a shocking reminder of a determined enemy and, in this case, my own inattention to what could have been a life-and-death matter. The image was of my mom and my two sons in front of our rented house. In the background was a red Toyota, with a guy sitting in it, watching his oblivious subject taking family photos on a sunny Athens afternoon.

8

□ □ □

PUTTING IN LONG and often irregular hours never bothered me much, so long as the work was challenging and I thought I could do the job. But my schedule back home carried an additional burden, imposed not by the agency but by my suddenly bifurcated family situation. My new position, training foreign intelligence and military officials, required me to travel abroad on a frequent and fairly regular basis. At the same time, I had vowed to see my two boys, Chris and Costa, every other weekend as was my right and obligation under my separation agreement with JoAnne. This particular labor of love wasn't easy. JoAnne had returned to her hometown of Warren, Ohio, where she and the kids were staying with her parents. So my routine became an exhausting high-wire act. On a given Monday, I'd fly overseas to tend to my job and remain abroad for ten days. On the second Thursday, I'd fly back to Dulles International Airport, get some sleep overnight, go to work Friday morning, leave work Friday afternoon, and drive five hours to New Castle, Pennsylvania, where my parents lived. By then, my folks had made the one-hour run to Warren, picked up Chris and Costa, and returned to their house across the Ohio-Pennsylvania border. I'd spend the weekend with the boys and drive back to my apartment in suburban Virginia late on Sunday. The next morning, it was time for the next flight overseas. This routine got very old very fast, but there was no other way if I wanted to keep my children in my life and still do justice to my job.

The job itself was not without its excitements and triumphs.

One day, for example, I got a call from our senior officer in a Middle Eastern country. "Listen, I've got an odd request," he said.

Let's call him Leo. Beyond this point in this particular story, I've had to change names, obscure or fictionalize countries, and alter certain facts; otherwise, it would not pass muster in the agency's publications review. But the tale still represents the kind of casework CIA officers abroad encounter all the time and the victories they record, which are rarely chronicled in newspaper articles or critical books.

Leo's request *was* odd. He said his people were running an agent, Abdul-Azim, whose real allegiance was to an unfriendly foreign government but who didn't know we were aware of his true loyalties. This double agent, growing suspicious, kept asking to see the head CIA man on scene, but Leo thought it was getting too dicey to meet with him. He asked me to fly out and represent myself as the new case officer in charge—the chief of our office in said country. That's what his real masters were pushing: They wanted their guy to meet with the agency's top man in the country, ostensibly to secure his direct imprimatur on the relationship.

I secured the appropriate approvals at Langley and contacted Abdul-Azim on my next trip to the region. The book on him at headquarters was that he was a local affiliate of a major terrorist group with roots elsewhere in the greater Middle East. To make matters worse, the guy worked as an engineer for a major U.S. defense contractor. Think about it: Here's a man who apparently wanted to do our country harm, and he's getting a paycheck from a major American company. You'd think those outfits could do a better job with their employee background checks. But I had to admit that we'd had some problems in that area ourselves.

The objective of our doubling him was to find a weapons cache that his terrorist group had stashed in this particular country and to identify others working with him. We arranged to meet at a hotel, and he seemed to believe that I was the new CIA officer in charge. He was an amiable, almost backslapping kind of guy, but he'd been very stingy about providing useful information since he'd been working for us.

I began by giving him little assignments—rent a post office box, get a phone number, identify a certain banker. His tradecraft skills were practically nonexistent. After every meeting, he'd immediately drive to meet his master's contacts and ask what to do. The assignments were harmless, so they always gave him the green light to give me what I'd asked for.

This went on for months. Abdul-Azim was increasingly comfortable with me, but it wasn't going anywhere. My frustration was beginning to show. "Look, it's time to fish or cut bait with this guy," I finally told Leo. "I don't mind flying out here, and you guys are all lovely people, but we need to come to some closure on this." Leo agreed. We needed to increase the stress level on Abdul-Azim, break him down a bit. I started to give him instructions on anti-surveillance techniques for his travel to and from meetings with me, emphasizing how important personal security was for both of us. "If you get caught," I told him, "you'll go to jail for espionage." But when it came to tradecraft, he was all thumbs, a real chucklehead. He'd get in his car at home and drive directly to his meeting with me; afterward, he'd get in his car and drive either straight home or straight to the foreign embassy that hosted his masters to report on our talk.

Meanwhile, his masters were whispering in his ear that I wasn't the CIA's senior officer after all. That started to make him nervous. Abdul-Azim was slipping into panic mode, looking for constant reassurance that I was who I said I was. Which, of course, I wasn't. We had another meeting, and he began to probe. "So you're the chief officer, right? You're not the deputy chief?"

"I'm the chief, Duke, the top guy."

"Okay, I just wanted to make sure, just wanted to know where I stand."

"You're very important to us," I told him. "You're dealing with the chief, the person you wanted to deal with."

He was still having misgivings. At our next meeting, he showed up early—fortunately spotted by our surveillance team as he walked into the hotel lobby. Before he got to the elevators, I'd reached him on his cell phone.

"Meet me on the sixth floor," I said.

"What room?"

"Just go to the sixth floor." Given the growing distrust between us, the last thing I wanted him to know was my hotel room number.

When he came out of the elevator on six, I greeted him with a bear hug that also served as a pat-down for weapons. He wasn't carrying. After a minute of pleasantries, I told him to wait ten minutes, then take the elevator to the thirtieth floor, just below the big penthouse suites. I went down the stairs to the third floor, waited five minutes, then took an elevator to thirty. He showed up a couple minutes later. "Why are you doing this?" he wanted to know. "What's going on?"

"I don't know who's following you; you don't know who's following me," I said. "This is for the safety of both of us." He wasn't happy, but he was on a mission and wanted to see it through.

My next order turned his eyes into small saucers: "Come on, let's take the stairs up to the roof. We can talk there."

"No, no," he said. "I don't want to go up there."

"What's wrong?"

"I don't like being in enclosed spaces. And I'm afraid of heights."

"Come on, man, what do you think's going to happen to you? We're wasting time."

We went back and forth for another twenty seconds before I grabbed him by the front of his jacket and shoved him into the stairwell and ordered him to start climbing.

"Please, please don't hurt me," he said with alarm in his voice. He went up six or eight steps, then paused.

I went at him again: "What's the matter with you? I thought we were friends. What the hell do you think I'm going to do up there?"

"You're scaring me," he said. "What are you going to do?"

"Look, do you have some kind of guilty conscience or something? You think I'm going to throw you off the roof?"

He was in an emotional bad place and it was time to back off. "Okay, let's go back down to the room. We're in room 3004."

The meeting didn't last long, given Abdul-Azim's unsettled state. All he wanted was out. He was barely out of the hotel before our techs picked up his call to one of his masters.

"Something's wrong," he said. "They're on to me." There were two or three minutes of excited chatter, with Abdul-Azim reiterating that his days as a double agent were over and the other guy on the line signaling his agreement. It turned out that they'd taken a picture of me as I left the hotel on a previous trip and were fairly certain I wasn't who I said I was. Abdul-Azim's handler wanted him to arrange one more meeting. At that meeting, he said, the agent would have only one thing on his agenda: His orders were to shoot me dead with a weapon they would supply.

I was scheduled to fly back to headquarters the next day. When I got to the office that Friday morning, the message from the Counterterrorist Center was loud and clear: There was no way Kiriakou was going back to that country for that meeting.

Of course I had to go back. This wasn't some heroic hot-dog play on my part: We were working with our host-country counterparts, and there was a fairly simple way to dodge a bullet, as it were, and still grab the guy. My plan was to post our host-country partners in the hotel room. I'd be in the bathroom, which was always right next to the door. Abdul-Azim would knock, I'd say "Come in" from the bathroom, he'd open the door, and the good guys would grab him. An easy plan, it seemed to me, unless he came through the door blasting away. But we knew he wouldn't; he was afraid of his own shadow.

Our partners pulled him into the room, took his weapon, and sat him down on the bed. He wasn't so much upset as he was angry. He

actually took umbrage at this assault on his dignity and spectacu-
larly lame tradecraft.

"You set me up," he said. "What do you think you're doing?"

"You stupid fool, do you think we don't know what game
you've been playing all this time? I thought we were friends. You
treat me like a friend and then you come here to kill me? What kind
of friend is that?" Yeah, I was laying it on thick.

"What do you want?"

"We want to know where the weapons are," I said.

"I don't know what you're talking about," he said.

"Where are the weapons? We want all your group's weapons."

"I don't know what you're talking about," he said, insisting that
he wasn't a part of any terrorist group.

We were getting nowhere, so our host-country partners took him
away and locked him up.

A few hours later, we reconnoitered with our host-country guys,
who were all upset because they thought we'd failed. We don't have
the weapons, they said. We don't have enough to charge him, they
said. Nice guys, but they weren't thinking clearly.

"You've been telling me since I got here that you think the
weapons are at his house because he has a maid who never leaves
the place," I said. We had to get into the house unnoticed, but how?

"Let's say there's a gas leak and we have to evacuate the neighborhood," I suggested.

"We don't have gas pipes here. We use propane tanks," one of
our hosts said.

"Fine, let's drive an eighteen-wheel propane tanker truck down
the street, leak some of the stuff on the ground, and you guys declare
an environmental emergency. Then we evacuate the whole neighborhood to the shopping center down the road."

Which is what we did. The house was empty, of course—no maid
and, it seemed, no weapons. But there was a safe, and we had a lock
picker with us. Inside, Abdul-Azim had stashed a map, leading to an

X-marks-the-spot location in an unpopulated area thirty miles away. We drove, we dug, we found—several boxes of AK-47 assault rifles and enough grenades to murder a small army. (Note: End of sanitized story.)

It wasn't the biggest score in agency history, not by a long shot, but it was regarded as a classy, successful operation, and it was strong enough in Langley's eyes to liberate me from the penalty box. *The Athens thing? Ah, just one of those anomalies. John's fine. Let's reassign him and move on.*

They asked whether I wanted to do "Greek stuff" again, this time from a base in the Counterterrorist Center at headquarters, and I said yes. Terrorism was abating in Greece, but there were still operations to do. I could reconnect with Radomir in that unnamed eastern European country, and I could work a Palestinian in London, a guy who treated me as a father-confessor. He had served time in a British prison and told me he had converted to Christianity while he was inside. "Seriously? You're a Muslim."

"You can't ever tell anybody," he said. "I'm a Christian now." Then he started to cry.

"I've done many, many bad things in my life," he said.

"I know, I've read the files on you. You killed what? Three or four guys?"

"I've killed thirty," he said. "Thirty men. Please, I must talk to a priest."

Through contacts in Britain, I set him up with someone who could really hear his confessions and offer him the absolution he sought. He wasn't going to get it from us.

MEANWHILE, THE GRAND Canyon between my professional life and my personal life was taking on new contours. The former was reborn in the spring of 2001; the latter was a continuing soap opera with plot twists absurd enough to win a daytime Emmy. JoAnne was the protagonist in this pathetic tale of revenge and bizarre behavior.

On June 8, 2001, I arrived at Dulles airport on a flight from the Middle East, skipped the office, and rushed to my apartment in Arlington, Virginia. I planned to shower and shave, pack a fresh bag for the weekend, and head for my parents' place in Pennsylvania to see the kids. My parents were going to pick them up around 6 p.m., and I figured to get over there later that night. This trip was special: I was supposed to have the kids for half the summer, not just the weekend; we had all sorts of things planned, including a visit to Disney World.

The phone was ringing as I got out of the shower. It was my mother, calling from JoAnne's parents' place in Warren. That is, she was calling on a cell phone *outside* the Tsimpinos house. "We're at the house," Mom said. "I don't want to alarm you, but nobody's here, and it looks like nobody's been here in weeks."

"Oh, my God, she stole the kids." It had just popped into my head, along with a vision of her returning to Greece and picking up with her secret life there.

I called my Ohio attorney, Mary Jane Stephens, who suggested there might be a logical explanation but that I'd best get to my folks' place in New Castle as soon as possible. "If you don't get the kids over the weekend, we'll go to court on Monday," she said. The road trip was a nightmare. Nothing I'd encountered as a CIA operative had ever frightened me as much as the prospect of losing my children; twice during the drive, I got so sick to my stomach that I pulled over to throw up at the side of the road. I kept calling JoAnne's cell phone and kept getting her voice mail. When I got to New Castle around 11 p.m., I tried to get some sleep but nothing worked. At 4 a.m., my dad came down to the basement family room, where I was trying to distract myself with TV, and asked after my state of mind. State of mind? I was a complete wreck and told him so.

"Look, why don't we get in the car and go over there, see what's going on," he said. So we did.

We arrived around 5 a.m. The grass was unkempt, reinforcing my mother's view that the house had been unoccupied for a while. But we saw a light on in the kitchen. JoAnne's dad always had trouble sleeping, so I wasn't all that surprised to see his face peering through the curtain on the kitchen door after I knocked. His expression telegraphed a certain absence of enthusiasm at the sight of his son-in-law standing in the shadows. Still, he opened the door a crack.

"Where are my children?" My tone was not friendly.

"They're safe and they're happy and they don't want you to be their father anymore," he said.

It took me a second to catch my breath. "That's not up to you to decide when they can see me and when they can't." Then: "How could you do this to me? I loved you like my own father."

He said something about how it wasn't easy living with my mother-in-law and his daughter. I was with him on that one, but it was beside the point.

"You're a party to the kidnapping of my children," I said. "If you don't turn them over right now or tell me where they are, I'm going to the police and report you." He lowered his head just a bit, said nothing, closed the door, and turned off the light.

At 5:20 a.m., the Warren, Ohio, police station appeared to be locked tight, but banging on a door roused a city cop, who opened up and asked whether he could help me.

I explained what had just happened.

"Do you have a separation agreement or a divorce decree?"

"No, we haven't been to court yet," I said.

"Well, then she hasn't committed any crime."

"Let me get this straight," I said. "You're telling me that if I find them and kidnap them back, I haven't committed a crime?"

"As long as there's nothing in writing, a parent is allowed to take her children. Or his children."

"Well, I want to report them missing." At least a missing

persons report would put something on the official police record, complete with a file number I could cite in the future if necessary. The police officer asked for the details and said that his department would be back in touch if anything—or anyone—turned up. Good move, I thought. Now what? *I know, I'll make maps of where all JoAnne's friends and relatives live and do surveillance. That way, I'll be using some of my CIA skills to track down where she's got my kids stashed.*

That bright idea got me exactly nowhere, although it did serve one useful purpose: It occupied my mind and got me out of my folks' house most of that Saturday. Then I had a real inspiration. My priest once told me that it's common for people with a guilty conscience about something to turn to religion. It was my impression that JoAnne had taken her faith especially to heart over the past two years, a period of time that included her relationship with "Uncle Stelios." By my reckoning, she almost certainly would be at her Greek Orthodox church in Warren the following day. Would she even consider going to church without the boys? The odds were a thousand to one against it: She'd be there, dressed to kill, with Chris and Costa on either side of her.

Saturday night, I called Pete Moniodes, an acquaintance of my brother from high school days—a big, burly guy who'd been a high school football star. I might need bulk and possibly intimidation for what I had in mind. My plan, as I explained it to Pete, was simple: "We go to their church on Sunday. We arrive late, while the service is under way, to avoid being spotted. Then we grab my kids and take off." Pete signed on and even agreed to drive.

We sat in the last pew and, sure enough, I spotted Chris in the second pew, standing with his grandmother. Alongside them was a man I didn't recognize; I learned later that he was Warren's chief of police, John Mandopoulos. JoAnne and Costa were nowhere to be seen. He had been fidgety, I found out, and JoAnne had taken him up to the choir loft in an effort to quiet him down.

I just stared at Chris, wishing him to turn around, and he did: He looked straight at me as I gave him a small, discreet wave. He didn't react and turned back to the front of the church. But every few minutes, he'd turn again and look at me. He was expressionless, which said everything: He clearly was not happy to see his father.

At a point in the Greek Orthodox liturgy where everyone kneels in prayer, I walked fast down the center aisle and said, as calmly as I could, "Chris, come with me." As I said it, I was reaching down to sweep him up in my arms. With that, he started screaming bloody murder: "Help me! He's trying to take me! Help me! Help me!" I took off at a run, not very graceful, given my eight-year-old son in my arms fighting to free himself. Several people in the church shouted at me to put him down and leave, but nobody tried to stop me. It's not wise to intervene when temporary insanity possesses a healthy Greek male.

Pete had headed for the car as I headed down the aisle, and he had it fired up and ready at the church door when Chris and I burst through. We piled in, just as JoAnne ran out, her face a mask of sheer terror. "Go, just go," I shouted at Pete, and we took off, heading back to New Castle on a crazy-quilt route of back roads I had plotted.

Chris was no longer struggling, but he was upset and breathing quickly. "Honey, I have to explain to you what I just did," I said. "Your mother was keeping you from me illegally. You're supposed to be with me for this part of the summer, and she wouldn't let me have you. And I came to pick up you and Costa." It came out in a rush. "Chris, why did you scream at me like that? And why wouldn't you wave at me when I waved at you? What's wrong?"

He said he thought I was a ghost. He said that his mother had told both boys that their father had been killed in a car accident. He thought I was a ghost.

Chris had calmed down; I was boiling inside, as livid in that moment as I had been when this same child had stared up at me while

I was shaving more than a year earlier and recounted his admonition to his mother about "Uncle Stelios." *What could she have been thinking? It was absolutely nuts. What would she do? Move back to Greece? Go to southern Virginia where her brother lived? Did she really think she could have a life with the children without my being a part of their lives?*

My angry and puzzled reverie was broken by the ringing of my cell phone. "John, this is Chief Mandopoulos of the Warren Police Department. I want you to return that child immediately."

"How dare you call me? I came to you yesterday, and yesterday your people told me no crime had been committed. Well, now I'm telling you no crime has been committed. This is my half of the summer. The children belong with me, not her. If you want anybody returning anybody, you tell her to return Costa to me."

"Now, I want you to turn around before this gets completely out of hand," Mandopoulos said. "You know, we're talking about some possible charges here."

"Forget it, Chief, forget it. You're the chief of police, you know the law. No crime's been committed here. There's no divorce decree, no separation agreement."

My former mother-in-law filed charges against me the next day—a class D felony for "aggravated menacing." Really, the statute is on Ohio's books, with conviction punishable by up to five years in prison. She alleged in her sworn statement that I had walked up the center aisle of the church, turned to face the congregation, and shouted, "I'm from the CIA and if anybody tries to stop me, it's going to be a bloodbath in here."

It was a family affair because JoAnne also got into the act on Monday, June 11, 2001, by filing a request for an emergency hearing on summer custody of the kids. My lawyer promptly filed one on my behalf. A hearing was ordered, to be held in a few days. Mary Jane, my lawyer, called me with some carefully chosen words of guidance: "John, as an officer of the court, I am not permitted to tell you not to show up at a hearing. What I am permitted to tell you is you don't have to show up at the hearing. And I'm also permitted to tell you that a court clerk called me and said that there's an ambush set for you and that as soon as you walk into the courthouse, they're going to arrest you and charge you with that felony."

I skipped the hearing. But word got around that there would be quite a show at the courthouse, and more than fifty people showed up. I paid twenty dollars to have the whole thing videotaped, which is a service the courts offer in Ohio, so my attorney had a visual record of the proceedings. Good thing, too: When my attorney announced that I wasn't going to show up for the hearing, a Greek woman slapped Mary Jane right in the face.

The judge verbally clobbered both sides for letting things go this far. Then he lit into JoAnne because it was plain to one and all that we had agreed to my having the kids for half the summer. She said she was deeply upset by my snatching of Chris. Could she have the children for one more day? The judge said yes, but one day only. "Then you turn them over to your husband." And with that, he dismissed the felony charge against me.

When my parents brought the boys to me forty-eight hours later, Costa rushed into my arms and cried, "Why didn't you take me, too?"

I was tearing up, too. "Honey, I looked so hard and I couldn't find you. But that's why I brought my big friend, because we wanted to take both of you."

We never did get to Disney World. Instead, my folks and the kids all came down to Washington with me and stayed for a while. I went back to work a couple of weeks later.

I'd been in a funk for more than a year, ever since "Uncle Stelios," the baker, and my informal probation—my time in the penalty box. Even rejoining the game at work hadn't snapped me out of it. What did was the entire tragicomedy in Warren, a clarifying episode that made me focus, finally, on what really mattered: ending a marriage whose only true blessings were two children so precious to me that I would fight in any court and in any divorce proceeding, if that's what it took, to ensure that their lives and my own remained as one.

This was the spring and early summer of 2001, months before the day that would remind all of us how fragile family ties can be and would change all our lives as far out as our shocked minds could imagine.

9

□ □ □

THE CIA OCCASIONALLY hosted visiting intelligence services from friendly foreign countries; the idea was to give them a tour of the Operations Center, get acquainted, exchange gifts, meet the director and some other top people if schedules permitted, and take some pictures. We wanted to make them feel welcome and important, and it wasn't a public relations stunt: They *were* important to us because they could be additional eyes and ears in places where our own access was limited by suspicion of the United States, language barriers, and a paucity of our own assets on the ground.

On July 6, 2001, we were hosting a group from a small Middle Eastern state; these were people I'd been training. The group included some relatively low-level military men—a colonel and a couple of majors—but I asked Cofer Black, the director of counterterrorism, if he'd stop by for a meet and greet. These guests were below Cofer's pay grade, but to my pleasant surprise, he agreed to my request. "This is a really big deal," I told my charges. "He's the head of counterterrorism for the entire world, which makes him a crucial guy in our shop."

Cofer showed up and shook hands all around, the model of diplomacy in such circumstances. When everyone was seated in a conference room, he formally welcomed them to the CIA and said how much we valued their friendship. Given his schedule, I didn't expect him to hang in for very long with these folks. He'd take a few questions, perhaps, then he'd be out of here.

But Cofer Black, who had a flair for the dramatic in his descriptive language, was concerned with more than diplomatic niceties that day. He came prepared and delivered a full and detailed briefing on topic A in his universe. The subject was al-Qaeda.

"We know something terrible is going to happen," he said after some preliminaries about the growing terrorist threat. "We don't know when and we don't know where. We do know it's going to be against U.S. interests and it's going to be big, perhaps bigger than anything we've seen before." Al-Qaeda, of course, had already hit American targets, including our embassies in Kenya and Tanzania in 1998, killing hundreds, and the USS *Cole* at port in Yemen, killing seventeen U.S. Navy seamen and severely damaging the ship. Its leader, Osama bin Laden, had declared war on the United States. Now, the head of counterterrorism was saying there were more attacks coming. The room went dead silent. Cofer had the full attention of our guests.

"The mood in the al-Qaeda training camps is one of jubilation," he went on. "We've never seen them as excited and as happy as they are now." Cofer said that the chatter we were picking up was filled with code words and phrases that our analysts regarded as frightening. "There's going to be a great wedding." "There's going to be a great soccer game." "The salesman is coming with great quantities of honey."

"These are all code for a terrorist attack," Cofer maintained. "We're sure it's going to happen, we just don't know where."

Then he appealed for their help and cooperation: "If you have any sources inside al-Qaeda, please work them now because whatever it is, we have to do everything we can to stop it."

The briefing lasted for thirty minutes or so and clearly rattled our visitors. Frankly, it shook me up, too. This was new to me. I hadn't been focused on al-Qaeda prior to this. Cofer invited questions, but no one responded. Finally, the senior member of the group stood up and said he would convey the substance of Cofer's remarks to his intelligence service; they would do everything in their power, he added, to help us.

The guys from the Middle East told me they were so shocked by the power of the briefing that they couldn't even think of any questions. But later on, I had a question for Cofer when I thanked him for his time: "Did you just make that up or embellish the state of play for their benefit, or were you serious in that briefing?"

"Very serious," he said. He'd been to the White House and he'd talked with Condoleezza Rice, then the national security adviser to President Bush. Richard Clarke, the counterterrorism coordinator in the White House, was also raising the roof, Cofer said, but no one was really paying much attention.

ON SEPTEMBER 11, 2001, I put on my best suit and drove to CIA headquarters, arriving at 8 a.m. or thereabouts. It was supposed to be a big day for me: Cofer Black and I were scheduled to go to the White House to talk to Condi Rice on an issue related to my current work—Greek terrorism. The U.S. Government Printing Office was about to publish a volume of cables between the U.S. Embassy in Athens and the State Department in Washington, covering the years 1948 to 1969. Most of the cables were innocuous enough, but CTC's position was that a few of them shouldn't be released because lives might be in danger.

I stopped by Cofer's office to tell him I was ready when he was; he asked that I check with his assistant out front to see where the car and driver assigned to us would be. It could be at any one of a half-dozen different entrances. She had the television on as I approached her desk, the screen lit up with an office tower on fire.

"What's happening?"

"Oh, an airplane flew into the World Trade Center a few minutes ago," she said matter-of-factly. It was the tone millions of Americans, watching early morning television that Tuesday, used when their regular programming was first interrupted that morning. Most everyone thought it was an accident, likely some amateur pilot who lost control or got way off course, or both. "Oh, you know, that happened in the 1940s, a bomber flew into the Empire State Building," I said, making small talk. "Funny, though, it's such a clear day, I wonder how that could have happened."

She and I were standing there, watching the television at 9:03 a.m. when United Airlines Flight 175 hit the World Trade Center's South Tower, seventeen minutes after American Airlines Flight 11 had slammed into the WTC's North Tower. Neither of us reacted at first. Then she turned and said, "Did you see that?" This time, the emotion in her voice was unmistakable. We both knew this was no accident.

I ran back to my office and alerted our team, then headed back to Cofer's area, where everyone was gathered in front of TVs. There must have been a hundred of us there, including deputy directors of intelligence, operations, and military affairs, and we were all transfixed by the images on the screens. Then, at 9:37 a.m., American Airlines Flight 77 crashed into the Pentagon. Finally, someone said what everyone was thinking: "It's al-Qaeda." And then someone shouted: "Will somebody please lead?"

It was like a slap in the face, and Cofer Black took charge, barking orders to senior and junior people alike and urging everyone else to get out of the building and go home. "Just get out," he said emphatically. There were still planes in the air, and everyone knew the CIA had to be on al-Qaeda's target list. A key bin Laden aide, Mohammed Atef, one of the planners of the African embassy bombings, had said back in 1993 that he wanted to fly a plane into agency headquarters. (A strike by U.S. forces killed Atef in Afghanistan in November 2001.)

I returned to my office and called Katherine, a CIA analyst who was my new girlfriend and soon to be my fiancée. We'd met in 1997, when she was working on Iraq and I was transferring to the Counterterrorist Center. I didn't see her again until October 2000, when I ran into her at a meeting, reintroduced myself, and invited her for coffee. We wound up talking about my marriage; she let me vent, proving to be a great listener and offering some gentle advice. I wasn't over JoAnne, but Katherine was patient. We dated on and off for eight months. Then, after the fiasco in Warren, she stopped by my office to ask about the Disney World vacation that never was. When I told her the whole story, she gave me a hug and a big kiss on the cheek. This could be serious, I thought, and I was right: It was.

Katherine was in her office when she fielded my call. "You should go home," I said.

"We haven't really had any orders yet," she said. By then, the CIA police, the so-called Security Protective Officers, or SPOs, were going office to office, herding people toward the exits. It took me an hour in my car just to get out of the CIA compound and onto the George Washington Parkway headed toward Arlington. Then traffic just stopped. I pulled my car off the parkway, locked it up, and walked home. Katherine and I watched the TV news; we could see the Pentagon burning from the apartment. We walked around for several hours trying to donate blood, but the Red Cross people in the area were overwhelmed. *This isn't right. We shouldn't be here. We should be doing what we can do in the best place we can do it.*

We walked back to my car and managed to work our way back to headquarters. We weren't alone: Everyone, it seemed, was straggling back, prepared to work all night long. We were getting names from offices and agents all over the world, literally thousands of them, and people were needed to do traces. Name traces normally are grunt work, what interns or newbies do, but the volume was just so huge that everybody in the place was involved. I'd sleep for an hour or two under my desk, get up, and do more name traces. Katherine was doing the same thing.

Everyone was running out of food, so a couple of guys from the Counterterrorist Center got bolt cutters and cut the chains off the doors to the CIA cafeteria. We took all the food, cooked what needed cooking, then set everything out on tables in the hallways. People could work, sleep, eat, or graze as they saw fit. The next day,

Marriott, which operated the cafeteria, agreed to stay open 24/7 for as long as the agency wanted.

But fairly soon, headquarters was not a particularly popular venue. It wasn't a case of nerves over a potential al-Qaeda attack. No. Nearly everybody was volunteering to go to Afghanistan and take on bin Laden's barbarians and their Taliban enablers. Here was another example of Cofer Black's remarkable leadership. A couple of days after 9/11, he summoned everyone in the CTC up to his office for a pep talk and a reality check. I don't think his remarks were recorded, but one part went something like this: "You know, we have a big job ahead of us. We're at war, a different kind of war than we've ever fought before, whether the country realizes it yet or not. We're all going to have to do our part. And not all of us are going to make it back."

You could have heard a pin drop. "I'm sorry to say this now, but we have to get used to the idea that some of us are going to die. But we have to do whatever we can to bring these people to justice. We owe it to three thousand of our dead compatriots. We have to do the right thing. And remember this, always: We're the good guys and we're going to win." That combination of truth telling and his willingness to take risks set Cofer Black apart from others at the agency and inspired the rest of us to believe in him and want to follow his lead. He richly deserved every accolade thrown his way.

People with military experience—especially special operations training—were in high demand; I had none of that training or those skills, save what I learned in the short course at the Farm, but I kept badgering anyone who would listen, explaining that I had other attributes that would come in handy over there. "Look, I've got Arabic, which is what these al-Qaeda killers speak, and I'll go anywhere you want me to go." The CIA guys who went in first, led by former U.S. marine Gary Schroen, who was planning to retire from the agency, were true heroes, the best of the best. Schroen came back, but Cofer was right: Some did not make it home alive—Mike Spann, for instance, a heroic former marine who died in Afghanistan in the early stages of the war there. What Schroen, Spann, and others did starting in late September 2001 made possible the air strikes and U.S. ground forces that followed. Our nation owes them an enormous debt.

My persistent volunteering must have worn them down. Finally, in early January 2002, I got a call from Dan Praig, a mentor and the guy who originally hired me for the temporary assignment that included Athens. "How's your Arabic?" He knew the answer because I'd been telling him and anyone else who would listen that my Arabic was good. "My Arabic's terrific," I said.

"Fine," Dan said. "Can you go to Pakistan soon? We need someone to take charge of counterterrorism operations there."

"Just tell me when, and I'll be gone."

The next day, I was on a plane to Pakistan.

10

□ □ □

AS SOON AS I arrived at our office in Pakistan, the guy I was replacing handed me the keys to a rental car and said, "It's all yours." He had been dispatched to Pakistan from his assignment in a Spanish-speaking country, but this was an abrupt handoff even from someone on temporary duty. No briefing on his cases, just adios, amigo, and good luck. On my first day, the deputy to Bob Grenier, our senior officer in Pakistan, said he wanted me to come up with a standard operating procedure for doing counterterrorist raids. I'd recently completed a course in advanced counterterrorism operations at one of the CIA's training facilities in the States; now, Grenier's deputy was giving me the opportunity to put what I'd learned into practice in a place reportedly teeming with al-Qaeda operatives and wannabes.

My plan called for raids that would begin at precisely 0200 hours. At 2 a.m., the streets of Pakistani cities were empty, and the bad guys, we figured, would probably be sleeping, too. Each team would include people from the CIA, the FBI, and the Pakistani military. We were in charge; the FBI was always supposed to secure evidence at the crime scene and the Paks were there for the obvious reason: This was their country, after all. We'd identify the house where the bad guys were and use battering rams to break down doors. The Pakistanis would go in first and separate the men from the women and children. Then we'd go in with the FBI.

When Grenier got word from headquarters that Abu Zubaydah was in Pakistan, probably in Faisalabad, I knew we'd need help and asked the Counterterrorist Center at headquarters to provide it. We

My grandparents, Yiannis (John) and Katina (Catherine) Kiriakou, boarding the Italia Line's MN *Saturnia* in Piraeus, Greece, in January 1931 to begin their voyage to the United States. They arrived in February 1931 and settled in Canonsburg, Pennsylvania.

THREE

Teen gets photo from shah, letters from world leaders

By DON NAKLES
News Staff Writer

Getting an autographed picture from the exiled shah of Iran surprised John Kiriakou of 307 E. Garfield Ave. but getting a letter from a world leader did not.

Kiriakou has gotten letters from other world leaders and it proves to him that world-famous people are human. "They have addresses just like everybody else," Kiriakou says.

RECEIVING A PERSONAL response from a world figure like the shah reinforced Kiriakou's belief that nobody is above corresponding, even if the writer is 15 years old and attending high school like Kiriakou.

He told his friends at school that he wrote to the shah and his friends thought he was crazy. "They couldn't believe it when I told them that I got an autographed picture.

"I got the shah's address from Time magazine," Kiriakou said. A story in the magazine said the shah had gone into exile on Contadora Island off the coast of Panama. "I just addressed the envelope to the island and the Peoples' Republic of Panama."

He wrote to the shah in hopes of receiving a picture or some other document he could add to his autograph collection. "I was so shocked to get an autographed picture.

After watching the shah's appearance on "60 Minutes" in which the shah defended his rule of Iran, Kiriakou became somewhat sympathetic. "I know he committed some atrocities but he was an ally of the West while he was in power," Kiriakou said.

IN HIS LETTER, Kiriakou thanked the shah for letting the U.S. use military bases and surveillance posts in Iran and giving Western countries oil during the Arab embargo of 1973.

The letter did not mention the world controversy surrounding the shah and Iran's present political situation.

In addition to the autographed picture, Kiriakou received a letter from the shah's secretariat. "His Imperial Majesty is now being subjected to such a great humiliation not only by his own people, but also by your administration," the secretariat wrote.

The letter and autographed picture of the shah will join an autographed picture of the Pope, photo of Cuban Premier Fidel Castro and Christmas card from Egyptian President Anwar Sadat as favorites in Kiriakou's collection.

Kiriakou has written to Israeli Premier Menachem Begin, English Prime Minister Margaret Thatcher, Queen Elizabeth of England, President Carter and King Hussein of Jordan. In response, he got at least an acknowledgement that his letter had been received.

LETTERS TO SOVIET President Kosygin, Premier Leonid Brezhnev and U.S. Ambassador Andrei Gromyko got no response even though the letters did not mention politics.

"For a long time I didn't write to Communist countries," Kiriakou said. The first Communist country he wrote to, Czechoslovakia, did not send a personal reply.

Only once did Kiriakou write a scathing letter of protest to a

John Kiriakou with autographed picture

world leader but he never sent it. "My mother tore it up," he said. Kiriakou's interest in short wave radios spawned his desire to write to world figures. He wanted to get something more personal than a voice on a short wave radio from far away countries.

"I don't write to be cute or get attention," Kiriakou said. "I just want to show that world leaders are people, too."

HE WROTE HIS first letter to a leader (President Carter) about three years ago. His interest in short wave radio has continued since his father bought him his first radio six years ago at a flea market.

The hobby includes writing to foreign countries to verify the broadcast of programs. He says he is one of only two people in the U.S. to write to Mongolia and receive verfification that he heard a Mongolian government broadcast.

Soon, Kiriakou expects to receive his 100th broadcast verification card from a foreign country.

In 1980 the *New Castle News,* my local paper, ran an article about me after I received a letter and autographed picture from the deposed Shah of Iran, Mohammad Reza Pahlavi. I had written the shah a letter telling him I thought it was a mistake for the Carter administration to withdraw support for him in the wake of the Iranian Revolution.

Standing with my sons, Chris and Costa, in front of the Parthenon in Athens. As much of a tourist destination as the Parthenon is, we never got tired of going there.

Port Authority of New York and New Jersey Detective Tom McHale in the office with a captured al-Qaeda AK-47. Tommy was one of the bravest and most patriotic people I ever worked with.

One of the vans stuffed with material taken from the Taliban "embassy" in Peshawar, Pakistan, after the raid there led by Tommy McHale. It was in this material that he found phone bills showing dozens of calls from the Taliban to numbers across the United States in the weeks before the September 11, 2001, attacks.

Tommy McHale (right) and me (behind him) with FBI agents in native Pakistani dress prior to a 2:00 a.m. raid on a suspected al-Qaeda safe house in Pakistan, February 2002.

These are computer-generated images of Abu Zubaydah that we created to try to get an idea of what he might look like with different disguises. We came up with dozens of variations, all based on a four-year-old passport photo we had of him. In the end, none was even close to what he looked like, and the images were of no help in his capture.

We captured dozens of documents, including these false passports, IDs, and credit cards, from an al-Qaeda safe house in Faisalabad, Pakistan. Many of the photos that were with the documents were of al-Qaeda members in disguise.

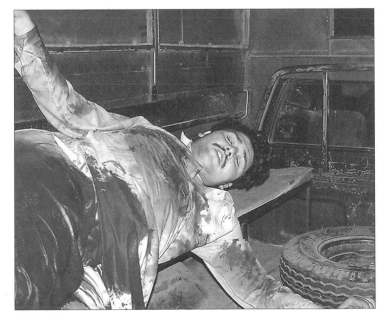

Abu Zubaydah's "bodyguard," a young Syrian in the safe house with him in Faisalabad, lies bloody and semi-conscious after being shot in the femur by Pakistani security forces during the assault on Abu Zubaydah's house.

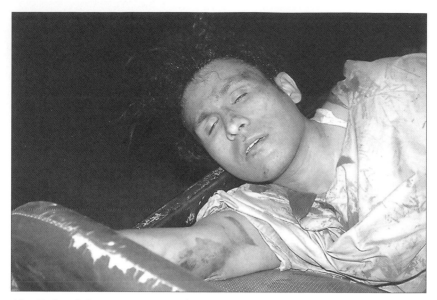

Abu Zubaydah, unconscious and near death, after being shot in the stomach, groin, and thigh by Pakistani security forces. Zubaydah had tried to escape by jumping from the roof of his house to the roof of the neighboring house when he was shot.

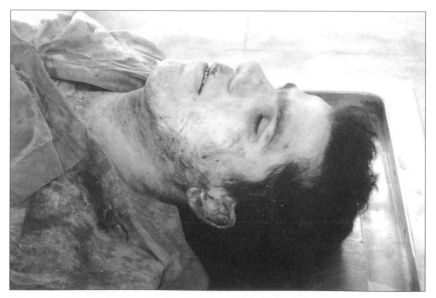

The Syrian bomber shot dead by Pakistani police in Faisalabad on the night of the Abu Zubaydah raid. The Syrian was building a bomb when we broke into the house. His soldering iron was still hot, and the plans to a western school lay on the table.

did get some "special help," but I cannot reveal the details because the information remains classified. My bright idea was to drive the streets of Faisalabad, hoping the special help would give us some clue to Abu Zubaydah's whereabouts; then, if we got lucky, he'd show himself and, of course, we'd recognize him from the photos we had of him. *Piece of cake: We spot him at the house he's using, reconnoiter, raid the place at night while the bad guys are sleeping, break down the door, and grab him. Yeah, that's how it'll happen.*

The fantasy of a CIA agent doesn't stand a chance of prevailing against the guile of a ruthless adversary. My bright idea was ridiculous: Only once in the two weeks did we get an inkling of where Abu Zubaydah might be, but the lead wasn't really actionable. He was very smart, moving around, covering his tracks in ways I can't discuss here, sticking to no discernible pattern. We used some fairly sophisticated methods in an effort to nail down his location. But we kept coming up empty.

That's when I told Grenier that we'd need more targeting help and a bigger team. I got Rick Romanski, the best in the business, and a group of CIA and FBI personnel large enough to get the job done.

AS I HAVE recounted, Rick used the reports we were receiving to narrow down the field of potential spots being used as safe houses by Abu Zubaydah to fourteen—all of them, it seemed, in Faisalabad or one other city. I'd never even heard of Faisalabad until I got to Pakistan, even though it's a city of nine million people and promoted as the Birmingham of Pakistan because of its large textile industry.

I first went to Faisalabad with Amir, the Arab American agent who was part of our team, to buy a house for our people during the Abu Zubaydah operation. The city was quite a sight: Every structure seemed to be made of hardened mud or unpainted cinder or concrete block. There were no tall buildings, not one more than ten or fifteen stories. Signs of poverty were everywhere, including an odor of rotting garbage and fouled water that hit you like a punch in the face.

People got around on overcrowded buses, motor scooters, trucks, donkeys and camels, and rickshaws—whatever was available. The place gave me one of those not-in-Kansas-anymore feelings: This was a very long way from home. I felt very small and very lonely.

But then, there is always something that brings America to you regardless of where you are in the world, something that demonstrates our country's global reach. Amir and I were hungry, but we were worried about finding a decent place to eat. We turned a corner, first spotting an open garbage pit. But not one hundred feet away was a gleaming glass-and-steel structure with a logo we'd seen thousands of times. Saved by McDonald's.

"I want a Quarter Pounder with cheese, large fries, and a Coke Light," I told the counter guy. Coke Light is what they call Diet Coke over there.

"Oh, why don't you try the Big Mac? It's better than the Quarter Pounder with cheese."

"No thanks, I want the Quarter Pounder with cheese."

"Oh, sir, the Big Mac has a very special sauce," the Pakistani said. "It will be to your liking."

"No, I want the Quarter Pounder with cheese."

"Well, sir, but the special sauce, it is homemade."

I was beginning to get a vision of this verbal ping-pong—my repeating the order and his defense of the special sauce—continuing long into the evening. "Buddy, just give me the Quarter Pounder with cheese."

He sighed. "Sir, we only have Big Macs."

"Okay, a Big Mac will be fine. Don't forget the special sauce."

It wasn't our only McDonald's encounter of the night. We made our way back to the other Pakistani city, but we got lost in the tangle of streets leading from our hotel to the safe house we had purchased a few days earlier. We managed to find the hotel and a McDonald's only two blocks away. Why McDonald's? There was yet another McDonald's quite close to the location of our safe house.

Think of these last two as McDonald's numbers two and three of what had become a very long evening. We figured the manager of McDonald's number two could give us directions to McDonald's number three, after which we could crawl on all fours, if necessary, to the safe house. But the manager was new to the city. Instead of verbal guidance, he gave us a map—sort of. In fact, it was the children's menu with a cartoon map on the back, with pink stars designating all the McDonald's locations in the area. He gave us a couple of clues and we were on our way.

An hour later, we were back at McDonald's number two, begging the manager for more help. He pointed us in the right direction again and Amir took the wheel with a suggestion for his colleague riding shotgun: Write down every turn we make so we can distinguish later the hits from the misses. There were no signs anywhere, so I was reduced to writing down directions worthy of Inspector Clouseau.

"Make a right at the traffic cop, the one standing on a raised platform with the Pepsi sign on it."

"Approach the big banyan tree and take a left."

"Go straight past the orphanage."

Finally, we got to McDonald's number three. From there, you could see the safe house, which we marked with a GPS before retracing our steps and doing it all over to ensure that our great success wasn't a fluke. It wasn't, but we both felt chastened and embarrassed by the experience. *Your tax dollars at work, good citizens. If we bring this level of tradecraft to the operation to capture Abu Zubaydah, we may wind up the laughingstock of global intelligence, as the guys who blew the takedown of one of Osama bin Laden's top terrorists.*

AS I SAID earlier, the Pakistani police and military people were strong players, especially Khalid. Actually, Khalid's ostensible boss in this operation was Mohammed, who was viewed by his men as a weak and uninterested dandy and who made clear to one and all that he wasn't happy with this particular assignment.

I met Mohammed once, as a courtesy, and dealt with Khalid on everything else. We were under pressure from headquarters not to reveal the name of our target to Khalid and his top people. The higher-ups were understandably concerned about a leak, and even Khalid himself wasn't absolutely sure at first that he could assemble enough trustworthy people to lead the Pakistani units on fourteen different raids. He ended up bringing in a kind of super SWAT team whose men dressed all in black, including a T-shirt with the outline of a 9 mm handgun on the front. With that, Khalid certified that his leadership team was leakproof.

Even then, we got blowback from headquarters, telling us not to share Abu Zubaydah's name with our Pakistani colleagues. Bob Grenier got very angry, which can be fairly intimidating because he's so good at maintaining his cool. "This is ridiculous," he said, when he learned that headquarters wanted us to stiff the Pakistanis. "These guys are prepared to shed blood for us. And it's the ultimate disrespect to tell them there's a dangerous guy and we want you to help us catch him but, by the way, we don't trust you enough to even tell you who it is. How insulting is that?" With Grenier's support, we told Khalid and his top officers that we had Abu Zubaydah in the crosshairs, or soon would.

We wanted to do a drive-around before our D-Day just to acquaint ourselves with our fourteen target sites. These were the houses Rick had pared down from the mosaic of numbers on his butcher paper. Most of these locations were one- or two-room mud huts with thatched or corrugated-tin roofs. But just as we were starting, I got a call from Rick, who was at our office in another city monitoring the operation.

A friendly intelligence service had just called, he said. "They got a walk-in this morning who said that a big group of Arabs from Afghanistan was hiding in a big distinctively painted house in Faisalabad."

"Can we talk to him?"

"No, they refuse," Rick said. "They say they'll pass along any relevant information. But no face-to-face. They're not budging."

Well, at least we'd be on the lookout for a big house with an interesting paint job. And sure enough, there it was, just outside the University of Faisalabad campus—site Y, the biggest house of the ones on Rick's butcher paper.

"I can tell you right now that there are bad things going on in that house," said the guy Khalid had assigned to us. "Look, it's the only house in the neighborhood with all the shutters closed." The house was clearly inhabited because there were outside lights on and cars in the driveway. "It's so hot," Khalid's subordinate said. "Nobody would close their shutters in this kind of weather."

"Well," I said, "we'll need a bigger team on that one."

Then it was on to site X, the empty lot I mentioned earlier that turned out to have an overhead phone line that snaked to the adjacent house where we found Abu Zubaydah on D-Day.

Back at the hotel in the other city where we had a safe house, we continued to meet with our group of CIA and FBI agents flown in for this special occasion. Unfortunately, some of the CIA guys weren't up to the task. We called them "glory hounds," and they were guys who couldn't cut it in the agency's clandestine service, but who had volunteered to go anywhere in the world where they were needed for temporary assignments. Many of them had something to prove: Mostly it was that they were wrongly kicked out, or had wrongly flunked out, of the Farm but that they were crucial to important operations around the world. One of them was particularly offensive to a Pakistani security guard standing watch in the hotel. One night, the guard tried to stop this guy while he was moving an unmarked pallet of weapons upstairs. There was a brief, but ugly, exchange of insults, and I had to jump in.

I intervened as quickly as I could.

"Wait a minute, pal, we don't talk like that to these people," I told our guy. Then I turned to the hotel cop.

"Sir, I'm sorry for my friend. I apologize for his language and behavior. But we're authorized. Everything's okay."

"I have to look in the crate," he said.

"No, you can't," I said. "Really, we have permission. You can talk to the general manager of the hotel about all of this. Please talk to him."

I knew he wasn't about to talk to the general manager; that would be taking on responsibility well beyond his station. He stepped aside, and we brought the crated weapons upstairs. Later, we'd transfer them to the safe houses.

Our disguises, such as they were, included shalwar kameez—the traditional, loose-fitting pants and tunic top—and the bushy beards we grew, or tried to grow. I have a dark complexion and a heavy beard; by D-Day, no one gave me a second look. My running mate Amir, an Arab American, had light skin and a scraggly beard. You wouldn't even know he was a Muslim. But he ended up looking reasonably authentic, too, perhaps a bit like a Taliban fighter.

On D-Day, our team gathered in the living room of the safe house at 9 p.m., or 2100 hours on the twenty-four-hour military clock we were using. A few days earlier, we'd brought in a half-dozen translators, so we had several Americans, including Amir and me, who spoke Arabic. I climbed atop a coffee table to brief everyone. "Okay, guys, I don't mean to be melodramatic," I said, "but we're going to have to synchronize our watches." In fact, it *was* melodramatic and, under the circumstances, absolutely necessary. Our drill required a strict timetable. The teams needed to be on-site at 0150 hours. At 0200 hours, they were to break down the doors, separate the women and children from the men, flexicuff all the men behind their backs, and grab all the computers, cell phones, and anything else that raised an eyebrow. By 0220 hours, they had to be out the door and headed back to the safe house. We knew we'd make a lot of noise, which put a premium on fast and professional execution. All but two of the teams got in a bus and headed off to Faisalabad, where the vast majority of sites were located.

Later that night, at site X, we had to sort out the chaos that attended the takedown. The bad guys included two Syrians and one Palestinian—Abu Zubaydah. All three of them had moved from the third floor to the roof when they first heard the battering rams hit the doors, and all three had been shot trying to jump to the roof of the house next door. One Syrian was dead when he hit the ground. The other was screaming from a bullet wound to the femur. Abu Zubaydah had three wounds and was unconscious and bleeding profusely.

When we got to the third floor, we discovered what this little group of terrorists was planning. The wounded Syrian was apparently Abu Zubaydah's bomb maker, and he was plying his murderous trade. Bomb components were arrayed across a table; a soldering iron was still hot. On an adjacent table was a map locating the British School in Lahore. These killers had selected a target—teachers and children, including a lot of American children. It made me sick to my stomach.

My orders were to take all prisoners alive if possible. One Syrian was dead. Nine others, who were never allowed up to the third floor and didn't even know the identity of its star attraction, were captured and turned over to our guys for interrogation in one of our safe houses. My top priority, under the circumstances, was getting Abu Zubaydah and the wounded Syrian to a hospital immediately. But the senior Pakistani security guy with us had other ideas. Abu Zubaydah apparently had killed one of his men and he wanted revenge. "We will fuck with him," he seethed. "Then he's going to die."

Not a chance, I said. "Look, I'm going to get fucked if he dies before we get him to a hospital. Those are my orders. This is nonnegotiable."

It was now 0230, and we had to move quickly. We heaved Abu Zubaydah into the back of a Toyota minitruck and followed the Pakistanis to a Faisalabad hospital. In a sense, my workday was just beginning.

11

□ □ □

IT IS DIFFICULT to describe the scene at the Faisalabad hospital. Conjure up the worst, most unsanitary and primitive conditions you have ever seen in an American hospital; then imagine, if you can, conditions in that hospital deteriorating precipitously and you begin to get some idea of what we encountered.

The hospital's doors and windows were wide open, allowing mosquitoes to feed as they saw fit. Of course, geckos perched here and there, feasting on the mosquitoes, but the insects had a huge numerical advantage, which allowed them to zero in on patients not protected by mosquito nets or simply alight on floors slippery with human blood and other bodily fluids. The odor wasn't exactly antiseptic. Medical personnel, meanwhile, had a novel method for sterilizing hypodermic needles: After use, a needle would be rinsed in tap water, then plunged into an industrial-size bar of Irish Spring soap. When time came for an injection, a doctor or nurse would pull a needle from the bar, rinse it again in water, and administer the shot to a patient. "This is like being in a nightmare," Amir said after we walked in, and he was right.

The doctors weren't expecting us—a bunch of Americans dressed up as Pakistanis, except for our bulletproof vests and weapons—and they certainly weren't expecting the kind of traumatic injuries we delivered to their tender mercies. Abu Zubaydah was bleeding out from his bullet wounds, and the docs had no choice but to do emergency surgery to clean him up, stop the bleeding, and sew him up as best they could.

Abu Zubaydah's cell phone, scooped up in the raid on site X, kept ringing, which would have given us a leg up if one of our Arabic speakers—Amir or me, for instance—had been able to answer it. But we couldn't; no one could answer it because the FBI agents, in their infinite wisdom, had tossed it into an evidence bag at the "crime scene." There it remained, sealed tight, outside of anyone's reach. I was not happy.

"Whose stupid idea was it to seal up the phone?"

"It's evidence of a crime," said one of the FBI agents.

"No, it's a communication device. The phone's not evidence of a crime. Everybody's got a phone."

"We can't open the evidence bag," he said. "It would break the chain of custody."

Those were the rules, FBI rules. I was in charge, yet I couldn't overrule and "break the chain of custody." But that was one rule that needed breaking. It was just so stupid. I should have opened the bag and snatched the phone. Worst case, some FBI knucklehead would have yelled and put up a fuss and that would have been the end of it.

We knew we had to get Abu Zubaydah to a better hospital. Security also had become a major problem. We had scooped up dozens of al-Qaeda suspects at all the sites that night, but we figured there were probably hundreds of others in and around Faisalabad. About two hours after our arrival at the hospital, we heard the sound of gunfire outside. Word had spread among the al-Qaeda types that we had Abu Zubaydah and we had him at this hospital. The bad guys were driving by and leaving a message with their bullets. Message received: We had to get Abu Zubaydah out of there ASAP. The Pakistani security guy assigned to us, a real pro, got on his cell phone and had a helicopter touch down in the hospital parking lot within twenty minutes. His people cordoned off the area so the shooters couldn't get near and we were airborne in less than five minutes, bound for what we hoped would be a better hospital.

Within minutes of our arrival, we wheeled in Abu Zubaydah, and the young Pakistani doctor took one look at him, shook his head and suggested, in effect, that the odds of this patient's living through the day were roughly equal to winning the big one in the Powerball lottery. "Seriously, Doc, he's got to live," I pleaded. "He's an important guy, and we really need to get him the best care we can." My orders were to tell the doctors to stabilize him as best they could, stop the continuing bleeding, and treat him beyond that only if a new emergency popped up. Our plan was to get him Western medical care as soon as possible.

Rick called with word from the director's office at headquarters: "It's 24/7, CIA eyes on," Rick said. "You can't leave his bedside." The doctor had left the room so we could talk and hadn't returned when I rang off. I grabbed a spare sheet, tore it into strips, and went to work, tying Abu Zubaydah to the bed. Then the doc returned: "What are you doing?" He plainly *saw* what I was doing, but his mind couldn't get around what his eyes were telling him.

"No offense, Doctor," I said, "but I don't know you and my orders are that this man cannot leave until we take him out of here."

"He's in no condition to leave," the doctor replied. "He's in a coma." Abu Zubaydah was unconscious and still bleeding, requiring one transfusion after another. But he seemed to be breathing regularly, although at an accelerated rate, and I didn't think I was jeopardizing his situation by securing him.

"Just as well," I said. "I'm going to keep him tied down." The doctor shook his head again, this time over the bizarre behavior of these American intruders, and left the room.

I just sat there, on a metal folding chair, and stared at Abu Zubaydah for hours on end. This hospital was far superior to the facility in Faisalabad, but its open-window policy was identical, which meant mosquitoes—very aggressive mosquitoes. I'd been perspiring. I'd been in the same clothes for two days. I was struggling to stay awake. In short, I was one ripe candidate for the hospital's entire mosquito population. At one point, I turned on every ceiling fan in the area to high, just to blow the little bastards away from me. It helped, but my exposed skin was slowly turning into one uninterrupted welt.

Amir was my savior. At one point, he called to ask whether I needed a break. "Oh, my God, yes," I said. He arrived a bit later and spelled me while I found an empty hospital bed and crashed for a few hours, not even bothering to get out of my clothes; then it was back to my job of watching a bad guy adrift in his own private twilight zone.

Another time, Amir phoned to ask if I needed anything. "Yeah, I haven't changed my clothes in a couple of days. I have one change of clean clothes back at the hotel. Do you mind stopping by and getting them for me?" An hour later, Amir delivered the goods and watched our package while I used the bathroom and changed clothes. Fresh socks, fresh underwear, and a fresh T-shirt: I would shower when I could, but for now, I was all set. The T-shirt was bright red, a Christmas gift from my kids, and it featured the yellow image of SpongeBob SquarePants on the front.

About two hours later, Abu Zubaydah began to stir. I got up and stood at the foot of his bed, hands on hips, just watching him. I must have cut an alarming figure, in my crimson SpongeBob T-shirt and my shalwar kameez pants, because Abu Zubaydah woke up, took one look at me, and registered pure terror. I could read his mind: Oh, my God, I'm still alive and the Americans have me. His heart monitor soared from 120 to close to 200 in a couple of seconds and began to beep-beep-beep-beep as if he was coding. A doctor and a nurse raced in and told me to leave.

"I'm not going anywhere," I said.

"He's in ventricular fibrillation," the doc said. By this time, another nurse with a crash cart arrived, and the doctor shocked him with a defibrillator. Abu Zubaydah's heart rate slowed, then steadied in the 110–20 range. They pumped a big dose of Demerol into his IV, and he was out.

After another four hours of swatting mosquitoes, Khalid showed up with his version of a care package—crackers and cookies, orange juice, and a few other items scrounged from vending machines at the hospital. It all tasted like a Michelin three-star meal to me.

Abu Zubaydah again climbed out of his stupor into consciousness, this time calmly motioning me with the fingers of his tied-down right hand to come closer. I went to him, moved his oxygen mask, and asked him a question in Arabic:

"What is your name?"

He shook his head from side to side and responded in perfect English: "I will not speak to you in God's language."

Fine, then, English: "That's okay, Abu Zubaydah, we know who you are. What can I do for you?"

"I need a glass of red wine." By then, the doctor was back in the room.

"What?" I thought sleep deprivation had disrupted my hearing.

"I need a glass of red wine," he repeated.

"He's hallucinating," the doctor said. I put his oxygen mask back in place, and they gave him another hit of Demerol. Sweet dreams.

I could have used some of the stuff myself. I was approaching two full days without sleep, except for the few hours in the adjacent hospital room and the occasional fitful naps on the metal chair.

A few hours later, Abu Zubaydah was awake, again indicating his interest in a chat. I walked over, moved his oxygen mask, and asked—in English—what I could do for him.

"Please, brother, kill me." He was crying lightly.

"Kill you?"

"Yes. Please, brother, kill me. Take the pillow, put it over my face, and kill me."

"No, my friend, nobody's going to kill you. We want you to live. You're very important to us. We worked hard to find you. And we have a lot of questions we want to ask you."

"Please, please kill me." He was openly weeping now.

"No, you got yourself into this situation, Abu Zubaydah. Now it's our turn. We expect you to cooperate with us." I put his mask back on, and he closed his eyes and went to sleep.

Sometime later, we had one of our last conversations. Amir had joined me and was speaking Arabic to Abu Zubaydah, who at first responded only in English and then went mum.

Then Mohammed, Khalid's boss, showed up with a bunch of his superiors—five or six very senior security officials. Abu Zubaydah went nuts. "I am not a zoo animal," he said, mustering as much outrage as a guy tied to a bed and struggling to stay alive could manage.

"Please, take it easy," I told him. "You're a trophy for them. They want a look, and now it's finished."

As they left, he beckoned me to his bedside and asked, "What is going to happen to me?" I thought we'd been through this, but maybe I hadn't been clear enough.

"Well, honestly, it's up to you what happens to you. If I could give you some friendly advice, I'd urge you to cooperate." At least I seemed to have his attention.

"You're at a crossroads right now, and you can make your life very difficult or very easy," I said. "You may be going to prison, possibly for the rest of your life. But you don't want it to be any harder than it already is. So, again, friendly advice: I urge you to cooperate."

"Oh, but I have nothing to say," he insisted.

"I submit that you have plenty to say, and you would be wise to share it with us."

"I'm going to die," he said.

"You're going to get the best medical care the United States has to offer," I told him. "You're going to get the best doctors in the world."

I knew we'd do something for him, but I was unaware of exactly what it would be and when it would happen. Then Rick called to tell me that help was on the way. Later, I learned that the director of the CIA, George Tenet, had set in motion a process that would result in the top trauma surgeon from Johns Hopkins Hospital flying to Pakistan on an agency plane. The plane touched down a couple of hours later, and we wheeled Abu Zubaydah out to be loaded up and taken away. I'd played nursemaid to this guy on and off for nearly two days and wasn't unhappy to see him go. It also didn't bother me in the least that he seemed to be terrified. As we moved toward the plane, he grabbed my hand and wondered aloud, "What's going to happen to me?" I think he thought we were going to kill him.

"Just relax, there's a doctor onboard and he'll take care of you." Then, he was on the plane. It was over.

Well, not quite. There were still the dozens of people we'd seized to interrogate. Apparently, al-Qaeda had given them an official story to explain their presence in Pakistan. *Sir, I came to Pakistan to study Arabic. A nice man in Abu Dhabi bought me a ticket and said I could study Arabic in Pakistan. My passport? Oh, when I arrived in Karachi, I wanted to give thanks to God, so I got into a taxi and told the driver to take me to the grand mosque. Unfortunately, I left my passport in the taxi, and the driver drove away.*

Dozens of guys, dozens of nearly identical yarns. Dozens of guys from Arabic-speaking countries coming to Pakistan, where Arabic isn't spoken, to study their native language. A visit of thanksgiving to the grand mosque of Karachi, where there is no grand mosque. That was their story, and each and every one of them was sticking to it.

Most of them were polite and well behaved, but we had one guy, a ferocious-looking Libyan with a multicolored beard, who meant to make trouble. His attitude was amusing to me. The Chechens had a reputation for being the toughest and most fearsome fighters in al-Qaeda. The Saudis were ideological purists. But the Libyans were generally cowards.

This Libyan responded to every question with "Fuck you" in Arabic. Then, when he was in a lower-level holding area with other prisoners, he started to chant "Death to America." The others picked it up, their collective Arabic voices making a real racket and beginning to carry outside the confines of our safe house. An FBI agent came upstairs, concerned that we had the makings of a situation that could spin out of control. I went down and told the Libyan to stop. Instead, he turned up the volume. He was flexicuffed behind the back, sitting on the floor with his feet crossed and shackled at the ankles. I put an arm under one of his arms and yanked him up hard—so hard that a prosthetic lower leg just popped off at the knee, still shackled to his other leg.

We were starting to load up these guys in a paddy wagon to turn them over to the Pakistanis. I dragged the Libyan to the truck and pushed him in. "If you don't shut your fucking mouth right now," I said to him in Arabic, "I'm going to take that leg and I'm going to beat you to death with it."

That did it. "Sir, I'm sorry, sorry to cause trouble for you," he said with tears in his eyes. "I've done nothing wrong. I am an alcoholic, I am a drug addict, I am a smuggler, but I am not a terrorist."

"Just be quiet and do what you're told, and everything will be fine," I said, closing the paddy wagon door.

I confessed my proximate sin to Jennifer Keenan, a tough FBI agent and one of my favorite people. Jennifer shrugged and suggested that I keep it to myself. But I couldn't; I had violated the rules and needed to report myself—perhaps it was an overreaction to my experience in Athens.

My second priest was Bob Grenier, the head of our office in Pakistan.

"Bob, I assaulted a prisoner," I told him over the phone.

"Oh, God, what happened?"

I told him about the chanting and my threat to beat him to death if it didn't stop.

"When did you assault him?" Grenier was still puzzling out the circumstances.

"Well, I grabbed him and pulled him up."

"Yeah, but you didn't hit him?"

"No, I didn't hit him. But I made physical contact with him."

"John, what are you doing? We're not reporting this. You're just asking for trouble if you put this in writing. If you do put it in writing, I'm not going to send it." As the boss, he had to clear all cables to headquarters. "Just take it easy and forget about it."

I WAS IN Pakistan for another two or three weeks, and it wasn't bad duty. We got high fives all around from everyone in the office for a job well done. Sure, we made some mistakes. We could have managed our logistics better. We busted one site that turned out to be a legitimate business run by a lovely old gent in his seventies who spoke perfect English. He and his two sons were hauled off for interrogation like everyone else, mainly because the information we had indicated that members of al-Qaeda had used his telephone. They had, but he knew nothing about their affiliation or objectives.

"I live in a very poor neighborhood," he told his interrogators. "When someone comes to the door needing to make a call, they ask and, of course, I allow them to use my phone." Our Pakistani friends checked out the story and found that he was telling the truth, and we had no reason to doubt them. It was an honest mistake, for which I apologized profusely on behalf of the U.S. government. The elderly man accepted with a kind smile, even before we fixed his door, bought new shoes for him and his sons, and made a financial contribution to his business for the trouble and embarrassment we may have caused. The next day, he appeared on Pakistani television, saying that the Americans had been very respectful, just doing their jobs, and that there were no hard feelings over what had been a simple misunderstanding.

On balance, however, our operation was a huge success. We captured dozens of bad guys, including one of al-Qaeda's topmost leaders. We worked well with the police and military of a nation whose help we wanted and needed. And we disrupted a bomb plot that would have killed men, women, and a lot of children.

Now it was time to go home. Katherine and I had planned a weeklong holiday in Santa Fe when I got back. But just as I was preparing to leave, I got an order to report immediately to another country, another front in the war on terrorism. Santa Fe would have to wait. I called Katherine, who still worked as an analyst for the agency, prepared to apologize and promise to make it up to her.

"Hey, don't kill me, but I just got this cable," I said.

She cut me off, with a smile in her voice. "Yes, I know, I saw it. Do what you have to do. But you owe me that vacation when you get back."

I did, and I made good on it, too.

12

□ □ □

ABU ZUBAYDAH WAS captured on March 28, 2002; at that point, I had been in Pakistan less than three months. Our operations were directed at al-Qaeda, but other American organizations were in the country as well, with other potential targets in mind. Indeed, by the time I got to Pakistan in late January 2002, counterterrorism officers of other government agencies in the United States, including some state and local types, had already begun to arrive. One of them was Tom McHale, a longtime detective with the Port Authority of New York and New Jersey. Tom was a cop's cop, a highly decorated guy who was in the parking garage of the World Trade Center in 1993 when the bomb went off in the first attempt to take down those buildings. He survived but spent weeks in the hospital and two years in rehabilitation; to this day, his lungs have not fully recovered from the toxic gas emitted by the bomb. On September 11, 2001, he was at the World Trade Center again; this time, thirty-seven of his colleagues died.

When McHale was tapped for an assignment in Pakistan, on loan to the FBI, he took it personally. The widow of Port Authority police officer Donald McIntyre, killed in the attacks, lent McHale Donnie's handcuffs. Tom used them anytime he captured a bad guy. "This is for September eleventh," he'd say to his prisoner, and he meant it. Tom had a great attitude, all positive, all can-do. In fact, once he got approval for an operation, he ran it with the kind of skill and professionalism that should make all Americans proud.

It began, as I understand from others who participated in the operation, one day in late February or early March 2002. Tom and a couple of colleagues were in Peshawar when they saw a run-down, small office building and one of them said: "You know, that's the Taliban embassy." It was there, rather than in Islamabad, the Pakistani capital, probably because Peshawar is on the Afghanistan-Pakistan border and because it would be less conspicuous. During the Taliban reign, only three countries recognized Afghanistan—Pakistan, Saudi Arabia, and the United Arab Emirates. "Every day they go and open that embassy," Tom told his buddies. "I feel like those bastards are rubbing our noses in it." But McHale wasn't just grousing. He and his colleagues came up with a hell of an idea: "You know what we ought to do? We ought to go in there some night and we ought to steal everything they have."

Tom got approval, and then began the detailed operational planning necessary to bring something like this to a successful outcome.

Like the rest of the Americans in the country at that time, Tom had to get the approval of the Pakistani government before he could proceed. The Paks reminded him that it wasn't much of an embassy—really, just a guard and one guy who served as combination diplomat and press officer. Apparently, these two men opened up every day at 9 a.m., sat around, did nothing, then locked up at 5 p.m. and went home. The Paks had no problem with the plan to raid the embassy some night so long as they tagged along as security and, oh yes, so long as their American friends made copies of everything for them.

McHale's boss, the FBI legal attaché, requisitioned several vans from the U.S. Embassy motor pool, and his team set out one night for the two-hour-plus drive from Islamabad to Peshawar. The operation lasted from around 11 p.m. until 3 a.m. The team just drove up, broke down the door, and walked in; there was no alarm. The place was loaded with stuff, and they took absolutely everything—computers, files, cell phones, weapons, everything that wasn't bolted to the floor or the walls.

It really made the day for one person in particular. This old-timer had bum knees, made worse by one hundred pounds of excess weight and bad enough so that he slept on his office floor one night when they gave out on him. He was an inside man, not an operative, but he had always wanted at least one raid on the résumé in his mind. When he heard about plans for the raid, he pleaded for a chance to go. McHale was a pro; he also was a great guy with a soft spot for toilers. The Taliban embassy operation could have gone wrong, perhaps wildly so, but the odds of it, given what McHale and his teammates knew, seemed very long, especially since the Paks would be there to provide protection. Sure, Tom told his overweight colleague, you can be a part of this one. Needless to say, it made the guy's tour.

After it was over, Tom told his bosses that the operation had been a success—no problems, no issues, all players present and accounted for. The bosses, of course, extended their congratulations and wanted McHale to send up a flare if he and his guys found anything particularly interesting in the pilfered stash. They didn't expect much; neither did Tom. At that point, the Taliban government was history, with its leader, Mullah Omar, and his camp followers in hiding somewhere along the Afghanistan-Pakistan border. But the computer exploitation experts went to work on the hard drives, making copies for the Pakistanis as promised and for certain U.S. government agencies. The originals of everything went to the FBI because September 11 was still an open criminal investigation.

McHale himself found something interesting and provocative. A file of telephone bills from the Taliban embassy revealed dozens of calls to the United States—to Kansas City and suburban D.C., to New York and Ohio and California, to Michigan and Texas, all over the country. For ten days leading up to September 11, 2001, the Taliban made 168 calls to America. Then the calls stopped. The file, amazingly, was in English. And here's the thing: The calls ended on September 10, 2001, and started up again six days later, on September 16.

This certainly was a matter for the FBI, or so McHale felt. The FBI team in Pakistan was alerted and got copies of the phone bills; all the originals went to FBI headquarters in Washington. Again, the calls were from a hostile embassy to U.S. destinations; McHale expected the FBI to be all over these phone bills and the addresses in the United States that had received calls from the Taliban.

By midyear, McHale was back in the States, resuming his duties with the Port Authority of New York and New Jersey. One day, he asked around to see if anything had turned up from the raid on the Taliban embassy; he was particularly interested to know whether the FBI had got anywhere tracking down the recipients of those Taliban phone calls. All he learned was that the originals had arrived at FBI headquarters, per instructions.

Flash forward to spring 2004. The 2002 Taliban caper was still gnawing at McHale—a bit of unfinished business that he wanted tied up for his own peace of mind. This time, having probed here and asked questions there, he had it on good authority that the FBI's people had never even *opened* the boxes of materials gathered up at the Taliban embassy. That, of course, meant that they had never examined the phone logs. Later, ABC News reporter Rich Esposito wrote about the story. Apparently, the FBI never opened the boxes because they figured they didn't have the language capabilities to translate them from Pashto, Dari, Urdu, and the other languages of Afghanistan. Still later, Esposito reported, the message from the FBI was that the information was too old to mean much.

How's that? Too old to mean much? A file *in English* of calls made prior to September 11, 2001, to the United States? Resumed on September 16? From the embassy of the government that treated Osama bin Laden as an honored guest? Maybe they were worthless, but McHale, for one, seriously doubted it. In any event, how could the FBI know that without reading them? Especially the file in English.

One postscript: After the raid that night, the Paks had asked the

Americans what they wanted to do with the press guy cum diplomat. McHale and his people had no further interest in him, and neither did anyone else. For their part, the Pakistanis couldn't have cared less. But they thought they'd have some fun and shake up the Taliban guy a bit—arrest him, then release him later. So they showed up when the guy opened up at 9 a.m. He was openmouthed when he saw what McHale's marauders had done to his office. The Paks moved in, cuffed him, and told him he was under arrest. As they were leading him away, he turned and shouted back at the guard: "Tell my wife to sell the car!"

Another postscript: In 2007 I ran into an FBI friend of mine at a shopping mall in suburban Virginia. We had served together in Pakistan and had stayed only in sporadic touch, but I still thought the world of the guy. "Whatever happened to those boxes of Taliban documents?" I asked him. He replied that it was like a scene out of that *Indiana Jones* movie. The files were still in those boxes, in an FBI storage facility in Maryland. Human eyes would probably never see them again, he said. What a waste.

13

□ □ □

THE AFTERMATH OF 9/11 left the intelligence agencies scrambling. We couldn't know on September 10, 2001, that we'd go to war in Afghanistan less than a month later. And we couldn't anticipate a war in Iraq that would begin on March 19, 2003. As a consequence, we were forced to improvise in one important area: the handling of prisoners. We had rules for the treatment of prisoners under the Geneva Conventions and the U.S. Uniform Code of Military Justice, although neither was invoked in the early months after 9/11. But we didn't fathom that we would capture hundreds and hundreds of enemy combatants—men who were not part of a recognized and uniformed army at war—and face the challenges associated with their interrogation. After 9/11, we were in a different war, the long war against terrorism, and there was no modus operandi in place for the treatment of captured bad guys, especially bad guys in large numbers.

That didn't mean we were operating with no guidance at all. When I got to Pakistan in late January 2002, and we started to interrogate people, our marching orders were fairly straightforward: We knew that we weren't allowed to hit anyone, to threaten anyone, to torture. To the best of my knowledge, we didn't violate those strictures, although some of us came close on various occasions. What became clear fairly soon was that it would be very difficult to get useful information from this new breed of enemy, these true believers in a radical cause for whom death meant religious martyrdom and a one-way ticket to paradise.

Still, violating even a terrorist's human rights and, potentially, the Geneva Conventions by resorting to torture is no small thing. And harsh methods, as torture is euphemistically known, aren't nearly as effective as their advocates maintain because most people will confess to almost anything, truthful or not, just to make the pain stop. You get information, to be sure, but its veracity is another matter. In practice, more empathetic psychological means, wimpy as that may sound, can yield much better results.

In the early part of 2002, as we were scooping up enemy combatants by the dozens, we were especially eager to find out where these guys had come from, how they had traveled to Pakistan, and what they intended to do there. Headquarters, interested in plugging holes, wanted us to figure out what routes these people had taken over or through the Hindu Kush—the mountains along the Afghanistan-Pakistan border. We had some success getting such information. But most of the time, we didn't get much more. It seemed that every detainee had that standard story about coming to study Arabic, although it is not the language of Pakistan, and losing his passport on the way to the grand mosque. Perhaps 30 to 40 percent of these people acknowledged that they had received training in al-Qaeda's Afghanistan camps, but to a man they insisted they were not members of al-Qaeda. Right, as if al-Qaeda issues membership cards.

For most of them, when we asked if they had ever seen bin Laden, they would say "Sure. I saw him at a wedding reception in 2000, but I never spoke to him and I didn't know anything about September 11."

So it went. Every once in a while, however, an enemy combatant would startle us with his candor. We had a Jordanian, for example, who freely admitted that he had been in Kandahar, Afghanistan's second largest city and the Taliban capital, on September 11. Our interrogation went like this:

"What did the people do when they heard that the United States had been attacked?"

"They danced in the streets and they jumped up and down and sang songs," he said.

"What were you doing in Kandahar?"

"I was working at an orphanage."

"Did you have contact with bin Laden?"

"Yes, I did."

"What kind of contact?"

"I went to the home where he was living and I pledged allegiance to him."

That struck us as an important admission from someone who hadn't been coerced in any way, and it prompted me to ask him why he was answering all of our questions.

"I'm your prisoner. I know I'm not getting out. It's not going to do me any good not to answer these kinds of questions. But I would like for you to listen to one thing I have to say."

During the interview, I was working with Tom McHale, the New York Port Authority officer. In addition, there were a couple of Pakistanis present.

"Okay, you've answered all my questions, and I don't have any others right now." I glanced quizzically at McHale, and he said he didn't have any follow-ups at the moment either. "Please tell us what you have to say."

"I would like to invite you into the embrace of Islam."

"You want us to become Muslims?"

"Yes," the Jordanian said, "it's the only way to save your souls. I would like for you to become Muslims and I will be your sponsor into Islam."

"Well, thank you," I said. "I respect your being honest with me. But I'm happy with my religion."

He smiled slightly and nodded. Then he extended his hands,

cuffed in front of him at the wrists, to shake our hands. That was it: The Pakistanis took him back to jail and we never saw him again. The episode reinforced for me and for Tom that tough-guy, in-your-face techniques with these particular prisoners might not yield nearly as much as earnest, direct conversation.

AS WE KNOW now, various arms of the executive branch of our government—the National Security Council, the White House, and the Justice Department's Office of Legal Counsel in particular— were wrestling with a central question: Given the assumption of significantly altered circumstances, was a new set of rules needed for the interrogation of stateless terrorists who had declared war on the United States and had already demonstrated a willingness to kill on a large scale? Other terrorist groups had expressed their enmity for the United States, but none had struck so successfully at the symbols of American power, and none had killed so many people. What's more, the attacks on the Twin Towers in New York and the Pentagon in Washington were only the beginning, bin Laden and his al-Qaeda propagandists insisted. There were many signs, recovered documents, and even some physical evidence indicating bin Laden's interest in acquiring weapons of mass destruction. If successful, would he actually use such weapons? The bet was that he would. In that event, did the old ground rules for interrogation make any sense when, say, harsher treatment of a terrorist might yield information that could prevent the death of thousands or even millions of Americans?

Abu Zubaydah's capture was something of a wake-up call because he was belligerent at the beginning and wouldn't cooperate a bit. Eventually, that would change, after we handed him off to the group that flew him from Pakistan to another overseas location.

At one point in the early summer of 2002, the Counterterrorist Center approached several CIA people with post-9/11 field experience and asked whether we wanted to be trained in what they called "enhanced techniques" for interrogation. We had some inkling of what these enhanced techniques entailed, enough to impel me to seek counsel from a top CIA officer I respected enormously. He suggested that these methods might well cross a dangerous moral and legal line, and I declined to be trained in them. Some of my colleagues accepted the invitation, and who could have blamed them at the time? Remember, this was still in the frantic months of mid-2002, when the prospect of another massive al-Qaeda attack, perhaps with biological or chemical weapons, seemed all too real. We needed actionable intelligence to prevent the next big one. Compared with kinder and gentler means of interrogation, these enhanced techniques of persuasion might get us what we needed.

The results of enhanced interrogations remained officially off limits to the public until late summer of 2008, when the Justice Department, responding to a court order, released a five-year-old report by the CIA inspector general on the alleged abuses. That sparked one of those eye-of-the-beholder donnybrooks so endemic to political Washington. Attorney General Eric Holder ordered a preliminary inquiry to see whether actions by Agency interrogators or contractors warranted a full criminal investigation. Absolutely right, said CIA critics, who insisted the harsh methods were illegal and had produced questionable intelligence at best. Baloney, said former vice president Dick Cheney, who insisted enhanced interrogation had produced actionable intelligence that prevented terrorist acts.

In fact, the report was heavily redacted, providing defenders and detractors alike just enough ammunition to make a modest case for their point of view. Cheney also repeated what had become something of a personal mantra: The Bush Justice Department had thoroughly reviewed the Agency's proposed enhanced interrogation techniques and found them to be consistent with national and international law.

Fortunately, we can take Dick Cheney's word and measure it against an extraordinary set of documents declassified in 2009 by order of President Obama. These are the so-called torture memos—the chronology of meetings and the legal rationale that led to the use of enhanced interrogation techniques, especially on Abu Zubaydah and two other high-profile detainees.

I'm not a lawyer, but you don't need to be schooled in the fine points of constitutional, statutory, and international law to recognize the deep cynicism threaded throughout the arguments made in the torture memos. Think Wonderland. Think a descent through the Looking-Glass:

"When *I* use a word," Humpty Dumpty said, in a rather scornful tone, "it means just what I choose it to mean—neither more nor less."

"The question is," said Alice, "whether you *can* make words mean so many different things."

"The question is," said Humpty Dumpty, "which is to be master—that's all."

THE STORY OF the torture memos begins not long after we captured Abu Zubaydah in late March 2002. According to a narrative put together by the Senate Select Committee on Intelligence and declassified by Attorney General Eric Holder in April 2009, the CIA believed in 2002 that Zubaydah was withholding "imminent threat information" during his initial interrogation. In mid-May 2002, agency lawyers met with their counterparts at the National Security Council (NSC) and Justice's Office of Legal Counsel (OLC) to discuss a possible new interrogation plan and potential legal obstacles to its implementation. Two months after that, on July 17, Director of Central Intelligence George Tenet met with National Security Adviser Condoleezza Rice, who told my boss that the CIA could interrogate Abu Zubaydah using the enhanced techniques, but only subject to a determination of legality by the OLC.

The United States was then, and remains today, bound by certain national and international laws and rules on the treatment of prisoners. We are signatories, for example, to the UN Convention

Against Torture (CAT), which seems pretty straightforward to me. In article 1.1, the CAT prohibits "any act by which severe pain or suffering, whether physical or mental, is intentionally inflicted on a person for such purposes as obtaining from him or a third person information or a confession." Then there is title 18, section 2340A, of the United States Code, which prohibits torture committed by public officials. Section 2340 (1) defines torture as "an act committed by a person acting under the color of law specifically intended to inflict severe physical or mental pain or suffering...upon another person within his custody of physical control."

The first of the torture memos, dated August 1, 2002, and signed by Jay S. Bybee, then assistant attorney general and the head of the OLC, takes on Section 2340 and basically argues that ducks don't quack and that apples are oranges if government lawyers say they are—that severe pain and suffering and specific intent are words subject to manipulation with a particular goal in mind. The memo is framed as a response to the CIA's request for guidance and plays back what the agency proposes to do under the rubric of "enhanced interrogation." By now, the memos have spent months in the public domain, and Americans and others interested in what is done in our country's name have become familiar with these techniques. But it's worth reviewing them in the context of the memo that gave them life.

That first memo, drafted in part by OLC lawyer John Yoo, describes ten techniques that progress up a ladder of intensity. On the lowest rung is the "attention grasp," a standby in station houses everywhere, in which the interrogator grabs his prisoner by the lapels or collar with both hands and draws him close "in a controlled and quick motion." Most of us could live with that, if the grilling went no further. But it does.

Next comes "walling," a logical extension of the attention grasp, in which the interrogator takes the individual in his custody and slams him hard against a wall built for the express purpose of making a loud noise on contact. "During this motion," Bybee writes in the memo, echoing what CIA lawyers explained to him, "the head and neck are supported with a rolled hood or towel that provides a c-collar to help prevent whiplash."

The "facial hold" and the "insult slap," rungs three and four on the ladder, are more or less what they seem to be—the latter designed "not to inflict physical pain that is severe or lasting." No, its purpose is to "induce shock, surprise, and/or humiliation." "Cramped confinement" is another technique that leaves little to the imagination: The detainee is kept in a dark space for up to eighteen hours at a time, depending on the size of the "container." The sixth technique, "wall standing" to induce muscle fatigue, requires the detainee to stand four or five feet from a wall, with feet spread to shoulder width and arms extended so that the fingers rest on the wall. The fingers support all the weight, and the detainee is not permitted to move or reposition hands or feet. Other stress positions can be employed, all of them designed "to produce the physical discomfort associated with muscle fatigue."

"Sleep deprivation," a hoary tactic used in interrogations throughout the ages, ranks as the eighth technique Bybee approves as legal in the August 2002 memo, although he cites conditions: "You [CIA officials] have orally informed us that you would not deprive Zubaydah of sleep for more than eleven days at a time and that you have previously kept him awake for 72 hours, from which no mental or physical harm resulted."

The ninth technique: Zubaydah apparently had a case of entomophobia—a fear of insects—so his interrogators sought and got approval to place him in a "cramped confinement box with an insect." The bug would be harmless, but Zubaydah would be told that his temporary boxmate was a stinging insect.

The last resort was "waterboarding," the harshest of CIA's enhanced techniques. Most of us know what waterboarding is, given the public furor it has generated since its use was first exposed. But

I think it's important and instructive to consider Bybee's dispassionately clinical description of the practice. "In this procedure, the individual is bound securely to an inclined bench, which is approximately four feet by seven feet," he writes in the memo, again reflecting what the CIA has asked that he approve as legal interrogation.

> The individual's feet are generally elevated. A cloth is placed over the forehead and eyes. Water is then applied to the cloth in a controlled manner. As this is done, the cloth is lowered until it covers both the nose and mouth. Once the cloth is saturated and completely covers the mouth and nose, air flow is slightly restricted for 20 to 40 seconds due to the presence of the cloth. This causes an increase in carbon dioxide level in the individual's blood. This increase in the carbon dioxide level stimulates increased effort to breathe. This effort plus the cloth produces the perception of "suffocation and incipient panic," i.e. the perception of drowning. The individual does not breathe any water into his lungs. During those 20 to 40 seconds, water is continuously applied from a height of twelve to twenty-four inches. After this period, the cloth is lifted, and the individual is allowed to breathe unimpeded for three or four full breaths. The sensation of drowning is immediately relieved by the removal of the cloth. The procedure may then be repeated.

According to reporting by *The New York Times* and others, the people pitching these enhanced techniques to the decision makers in the White House and Justice Department had no sense of their provenance. They apparently did not know that waterboarding was a form of torture favored by interrogators during the Spanish Inquisition and, more recently, by the Communists during the Korean War. The common thread was motive: In fifteenth- and sixteenth-century Spain and twentieth-century Korea, the interrogators sought conversions or false confessions that could be used for propaganda purposes.

The Korean experience is why the U.S. military now uses versions of enhanced interrogation techniques on pilots and special operations personnel in a program called SERE, for Survival, Evasion, Resistance, and Escape. Our government wants to give our people a sampling of what they might have to endure if they are captured and interrogated by an enemy inattentive to the fine points of the UN Convention Against Torture. But there is one big difference between what our pilots and special ops people undergo and what we do to detainees under our control: Our folks know that SERE, as tough as it is, is still a training exercise. In contrast, the entire point of enhanced interrogation on detainees is to convince them that it's real—physical and mental anguish without finite end. The whole idea is to induce a sense of hopelessness, cut short only if they choose the option of cooperation with their tormentors.

In the Bybee memo, and in three others from May 2005 signed by the OLC's Steven G. Bradbury, the lawyers argue that none of these enhanced interrogation techniques, used separately or in combination, amount to torture as CIA advocates have attested to them. The reasoning turns on the parsing of some key words. Throughout the memos and their antiseptic descriptions of what is proposed for recalcitrant detainees, great weight is accorded to the fact that medical and psychological personnel would be on hand to monitor the administration of each and every enhanced technique. The medical doctors and shrinks would safeguard the process, presumably by spotting the precise moment mere physical or mental pain or suffering is about to graduate to "severe," thus becoming torture and violating the law. Even past that point, the action might not clear the bar and qualify as torture if the interrogator had not "specifically intended" it as such.

By the time the last memo was signed by Bradbury on

May 30, 2005, the hierarchy of enhanced techniques had grown to fourteen, with waterboarding still atop the pyramid as the interrogators' last, best option. Now, having argued that none of these techniques can be construed as torture so long as the interrogators are careful about the severity and intent of their actions, the lawyers focus on what I think may be the ultimate loophole: jurisdiction.

Abu Zubaydah, Khalid Shaikh Mohammed, and Abd al-Rahim al-Nashiri, the third detainee waterboarded, were all captured abroad and interrogated in foreign countries. As it happens, article 16 of the UN Convention Against Torture places no obligation on a signatory state for acts outside "territory under its jurisdiction." Presto: no jurisdiction, no obligation under CAT.

The memo also raises a U.S. Senate "reservation" placed on our signing of the CAT. We would be bound by the convention only insofar as the phrase "cruel, inhuman or degrading treatment or punishment" meant those words as prohibited by the Fifth, Eighth, and/or Fourteenth amendments to the U.S. Constitution. Fair enough, you and I could live with that, right? We could, but the lawyers can't. "These Amendments," the OLC lawyers insist in their guidance to the CIA, "have been construed by the courts not to extend protections to aliens outside the United States." You get the idea.

Waterboarding, then Vice President Cheney said publicly, was fine with him as an interrogation technique used against America's enemies, even as the Bush administration officially insisted that our nation does not torture. I wonder whether Cheney would regard waterboarding as torture if al-Qaeda or Taliban terrorists applied it to our country's brave men and women fighting in Afghanistan. Or, for that matter, if waterboarding were combined with sleep deprivation, stress positions, and the other fun-house horrors and used against a relative or close friend.

The lawyers can play their word games, but there's no real

mystery here. We know what torture is. It's waterboarding that triggers a gag reflex and sense of suffocation, induces vomiting, and causes extreme stomach pain because of the stress on the abdominal muscles. It's sleep deprivation that keeps a prisoner awake for days on end, then allows for no more than eight hours of sleep before the cycle begins again. It's the use of these and other methods designed to force information from a detainee who is likely to say anything just to make the regime of pain and suffering end, even if some tame doctor rules it less than "severe."

Let's stipulate for the sake of argument that such practices produce a desired result. Different intelligence arms of our government may not always agree that a specific interrogation produced actionable information.

But even if torture works, it cannot be tolerated—not in one case or a thousand or a million. If their efficacy becomes the measure of abhorrent acts, all sorts of unspeakable crimes somehow become acceptable. Barack Obama got it right when he declassified the OLC memos of 2002 and 2005: "Torture," the president of the United States said, "corrodes the character of a country."

14

□ □ □

EVEN THOUGH ENHANCED techniques were supposed to be used only on the highest-profile, toughest, most important al-Qaeda prisoners, word of their existence got out pretty quickly. By this time, we had already invaded Iraq, and military interrogators there—including a few agency contractors—were using these harsh methods, and some gruesomely inhumane variations of them, on their prisoners. The military wasn't bound by a presidential finding approving the techniques or by an agreement negotiated between the agency and the Justice Department. There was no oversight and no accountability, which meant interrogation was destined to spin out of control. The result was Abu Ghraib, a dark stain on the U.S. Army and, because some CIA contractors were involved, on the agency as well.

Then there was Guantánamo, which posed a special challenge for U.S. interrogators, military and nonmilitary. Our forces were picking up large numbers of combatants, or people identified as combatants, in Afghanistan during the first six months of the U.S. presence there. At first, a prison was opened at Bagram Air Base in Afghanistan. It was pretty grisly and filled up fast. With the numbers building, Guantánamo became a logical place to consider as an additional detention center. In my view, the original idea was a good one. This was an unconventional war with unconventional detainees, many of whom may not have even committed crimes. The United States and its allies had to put them somewhere while their status was determined.

Guantánamo allowed us, we thought, to park a prisoner for a

limited period of time until we could get to the bottom of his story. Then he could be either released to his home country or put on trial. I don't think anybody had any idea that hundreds of prisoners, many of them innocent, would spend years of their lives in political and legal limbo in Cuba, with no right to trial and no review of their cases. As I see it, this was not the original intent of Guantánamo and is yet another stain on the Bush administration's complete failure to come up with a policy on detention and interrogation and then to stick with it. The original intent was good. The result was a national disgrace.

The mistake made early on was sending just about everyone to Gitmo. American troops and their allies were capturing shepherds and mechanics and opium farmers. What to do? Send them to Guantánamo. Compounding this mistake was a U.S. government program that paid a bounty to the Northern Alliance, the coalition of Afghan tribes that worked with the CIA and U.S. Special Forces to bring down the Taliban, for every foreigner turned over to American forces. At the time, there were plenty of foreigners in Afghanistan who were just minding their own business, including many Pakistanis. For that matter, there were plenty of Afghans, unaffiliated with the Northern Alliance, who fell into the same category. Members of the alliance would grab these people, turn them over to the U.S. military, and claim they were terrorists. Then it was off to Guantánamo.

The place was overfilled because the Americans took at face value what the Northern Alliance was telling us. We would have been much better off keeping the Afghans in Afghanistan and sending the Pakistanis home to be interrogated in their own country. Indeed, that was something I pushed for when I was in Pakistan. I thought Pakistanis we caught in our various raids ought to be turned over to Pakistani authorities, and Afghans should be turned over to the Afghans. It made no sense to me to capture a Pakistani in Pakistan, for example, and then take him out of Pakistan and eventually ship him to Guantánamo. Besides, turning those prisoners over to their governments would have freed up more space in Guantánamo for the real al-Qaeda people we were catching.

There was also the problem of high-profile prisoners. Should their American wardens send them to Guantánamo? It didn't seem feasible. First, the facility was full. Second, detainees there were living in contained but open areas—in effect, large cages visible to one and all. Assuming that some of the prisoners would recognize, say, Abu Zubaydah or Khalid Shaikh Mohammed, the custodians of Guantánamo could end up with a riot on their hands.

Abu Zubaydah, the first major al-Qaeda figure captured, was the obvious test case. He was found in Pakistan, where we had no reliable facility to imprison him and where his medical condition might not get the highly skilled attention the agency wanted for him. He couldn't be shipped to Afghanistan, where prison conditions were terrible. That's when agency brass began to think about the possibility of third countries for these high-profile al-Qaeda types. The negotiations were so tightly held that perhaps only a half-dozen CIA people knew about them at the time. The operation had a code name—let's give it the fictitious label "Emerald" here. Emerald was a military facility, the first of the secret prisons—"black sites" in the vernacular—where top al-Qaeda people were shipped for interrogation after their capture. Abu Zubaydah was Emerald's first occupant.

Prisons were set up in other countries as well. Each secret facility housed a relatively small number of prisoners, each of them isolated from all the others. In some cases, enhanced techniques were used, but only by authorized CIA personnel and generally in combination with low-key, more conversational methods—bad cop, good cop, if you will, generally in accordance with the *U.S. Army Field Manual* on interrogation. At least that's what we were led to believe at the time.

It's difficult to keep anything secret in Washington and in the

U.S. government. Inevitably, word of these offshore facilities found its way into the press.

But our concerns weren't focused solely on these top-tier enemy combatants. Another group filling Guantánamo and Afghan facilities included somewhat lower-profile detainees, perceived to have far less information of value to our antiterrorism efforts. Many of these enemy combatants, after questioning by our people, were returned to their countries of origin—Egyptians to Egypt, Saudis to Saudi Arabia, and so on. The process, known as "rendition" because it fit the legal definition of turning over a person from one entity or jurisdiction to another, generated a lot of controversy when it went public in the press.

The attention was hardly surprising. These detainees were being passed along to governments and intelligence services not known for their gentle treatment of your average street protester, much less someone who had admitted to having been trained by al-Qaeda. I confess to some ambivalence about rendition, extraordinary—that is, without a formal legal proceeding—or otherwise. Most of these people were trained in one of al-Qaeda's camps to kill Americans. We didn't want to keep them in Afghanistan because they weren't Afghans. And many of them hadn't even committed a crime in Afghanistan. Why is it wrong for us to ship them back to their native countries? Even though these prisoners might be treated harshly back home, I had no problem with rendition. I had a tougher time caring about these guys. Should we send them to Guantánamo, where they get three squares a day and better medical care than half of America? I had a problem with *that*. We obviously made some mistakes—for example, sending a guy to the tougher of the two countries when he had dual citizenship. But as I understand it, these mistakes were few and far between. Most prisoners rendered to home countries wound up being released after relatively short periods of detention.

But the issue of rendition needs to be seen in a larger context.

Someone in the Bush administration—former defense secretary Donald Rumsfeld, I believe—once worried aloud about whether we could kill the terrorists faster than their leaders and religious enablers could churn out new recruits. However crudely he put it, Rumsfeld was touching on an important point. Bin Laden and his support system in madrassas and conservative Islamic societies attract recruits with a devil's mix of Muslim victimization, radical Islam, false promises, and the vision of a reborn caliphate spreading across the Near East, Middle East, and beyond. These young men, effectively brainwashed, march forward like robotic figures in some video game, fighting Americans in Afghanistan, conducting suicide bombings where they can, and otherwise responding to the instructions of their masters.

We can wage war against this irregular army of lunatics, and we can certainly kill a lot of them. But we also know, as some top U.S. military officers have acknowledged, that the larger challenge is to win hearts and minds—to win an epic conflict fought on moral and political battlefields. I've come around to the view that, while we must do everything we can to prevent terrorists from attacking us, we also need to wage war on these other battlefields, where the force of our ideas matters as much as, if not more, than our force of arms.

You cannot have grown up as I did, in a household that revered the United States and what it stands for, and not believe in American exceptionalism. Our country salutes more than martial music and the flag. We also pledge fealty to what "Stars and Stripes Forever" represents: our written Constitution and our belief in standards of behavior that set an example for people and cultures everywhere on Earth.

There are things we should not do, even in the name of national security. One of them, I now firmly believe, is torture.

15

□ □ □

WHEN I RETURNED from Pakistan in late spring 2002, I took up an assignment as a branch chief in the Counterterrorist Center's Osama bin Laden unit, a group set up in the mid-1990s to focus on the terrorist's increasingly brutal activities. The spot was something of a placeholder until Bob Grenier returned to headquarters from his work in Pakistan. Bob had been promoted to associate deputy director of operations for policy support, a mouthful of a title that hadn't existed before because the job itself hadn't existed. Grenier needed an executive assistant; he thought I'd done well in Pakistan, and I was flattered when he chose me for his new team. Both of us, though, were a bit baffled by our marching orders or, more precisely, the lack of them. There was no job description, but Bob took "policy support" to mean what the words said—that he would be the agency's counterterrorism liaison to the White House and to the larger policy community that included the Departments of Defense and State, as well as the appropriate committees of Congress.

My first day on the job was August 1, 2002, and it was a bracing eye-opener to say the least. After we exchanged a few pleasantries and reminiscences about Pakistan, Bob told me we had to go upstairs to be read into a compartment—that is, a zone of CIA business or an agency decision so secret that knowledge of it was limited to a small subset of people.

"What compartment?"

"I don't know," Grenier said. "It's apparently so sensitive that they won't even discuss it over the phone. They won't tell us anything until we sign the secrecy document." This was unusual, though not unprecedented: Waterboarding had been a compartmented decision, with only a few people in the know.

Upstairs was the floor where Iraq operations were quartered. We went into the office of the director. I cannot use his name here for security reasons.

"What is this?" It wasn't an angry question; Bob was interested in *some* hint of the activity or decision before signing documents. That seemed a reasonable position to me as well.

"I can't say anything until you sign the secrecy agreements," the director said. We signed six of them, just page after page after page of secrecy agreements. The agency sometimes goes overboard on this sort of thing. For all we knew at that moment, we'd just agreed to never reveal the identity of the new bottled-water vendor supplying the CIA cafeteria.

Our host was finally satisfied as we checked off the last page.

"Okay, here's the deal," he said. "We're going to invade Iraq next spring. We're going to overthrow Saddam Hussein. We're going to establish the largest air force base in the world, and we're going to transfer everybody from Saudi Arabia to Iraq. That way, al-Qaeda won't have that hanging over us, that we're polluting the land of the two holy cities."

His reference to holy cities reflected a dilemma that had its roots in a decade-old conflict. Remember Operation Desert Shield? After Iraq's invasion of Kuwait in August 1990, we were concerned about Saddam's possible designs on Saudi Arabia. Desert Shield led to a massive American presence in Saudi Arabia that included air bases, hundreds of thousands of ground troops, and the enormous logistical support that attends such war-making enterprises. Our men and women were there as a clear sign to Saddam Hussein that the United States and its coalition meant business when they threatened Iraq with war if its invasion of Kuwait and its implicit threat to Saudi Arabia were not reversed. The subsequent Operation Desert Storm, which began in January 1991, effectively destroyed Saddam's air force and clobbered his armies, sending them back to Baghdad, tails between their legs.

Afterward, however, a significant U.S. military presence remained in Saudi Arabia, at the grateful invitation of the royal family. This had been a significant sticking point with the Saudi-born bin Laden. His catalog of alleged U.S. sins was long: its unwavering support for Israel, its occupation of Palestinian lands, and its backing of autocratic governments in the Middle East. But garrisoning infidel forces in the land of Mecca and Medina was beyond the pale for the al-Qaeda leader. If the United States left Saudi Arabia, it would release some of the tension in the region.

Grenier wasn't concerned about that: "We're going to invade Iraq?" He was cool as usual, and I wasn't quite sure whether he was stating the fact or asking a rhetorical question. I was incredulous. How could anyone not be?

"It's a done deal, Bob," our host said. "The decision's already been made."

"Isn't this premature?" Grenier asked. "We haven't captured bin Laden yet."

"No matter, the planning's completed, everything's in place." The idea, our host went on, is to ratchet up the pressure on weapons of mass destruction—keep in mind, everyone thought Saddam had them then. We'd go to the United Nations toward the end of the year to make it look as if we wanted to ask the UN Security Council to authorize force. We expected Russian, Chinese, and French opposition, he said, and we were prepared to go it alone.

This was dumbfounding. Here was someone at the CIA, obviously plugged into the plans of the executive branch, telling us that the public debate in Congress, reflected almost daily in the press, meant nothing: We were going to war regardless of what the legislative branch of the federal government chose to do. We just sat there, wondering what the hell they were thinking over in the White

House. And what was he suggesting about the CIA's place in this evolving story? Was this going to be like Afghanistan? Was he telling us this because the agency would again be in the lead—the tip of the spear in an invasion of Iraq? Maybe our host was a mind reader or maybe it was an accident of timing in his script, but he went directly to my unasked question:

"Our role is going to be one of support," he said. "It's not going to be a rerun of Afghanistan, where we were running the show." He reiterated that there would be no turning back: The decision had been made. Just as an aside, the support he mentioned apparently had some odd and even presumptuous components. Once, when I walked into this guy's office for another meeting, I found him at his desk with a bunch of multicolored Magic Marker pens, redesigning the Iraqi flag. At one point, he was using sky blue and white, a bizarre choice in the extreme, given that those are the colors of the Israeli national flag—and, I should add, the Greek flag, too. In any event, you would have thought we'd leave the chore of designing their flag to the Iraqis themselves. The Iraqis did get rid of the old Saddam-era flag and replaced it, in January 2008, with a flag of three horizontal stripes—red, white, and black to reflect Arab liberation colors—with green Arabic script in the white panel with the phrase "God is great."

As we left the erstwhile flag designer's office that first time and headed for our own, I was shaking my head in disbelief. Bob was just shaking his head, as well, a bemused expression clouding his face. Later, he told me that one of his bosses at the agency had briefed him on the executive branch's thinking a couple of months earlier.

"This is crazy," I said. "You know how busy we were in Pakistan? You know how busy the next year's going to be? It'll be hell."

"I'm not even sure how to proceed here," Bob said. "Right now, we're a staff of exactly two. How are we going to organize ourselves?" *Pretty simple, really, you're the boss, and I work for you.*

Between us, we'll end up working eighty to one hundred hours a week and get half the job done. The long hours are okay; it's the prospect of not finishing the job that hurts.

Later that day, Bob heard from his boss, the deputy director of operations, who apparently had signed the secrecy papers, too, because he phoned specifically to name Bob the Iraq mission manager. That meant Bob Grenier would be the agency's face to the rest of the Washington community on everything having to do with Iraq. Bob would have direct access to the director of central intelligence, George Tenet. If anybody wanted anything done by the CIA, Bob was the go-to guy.

WE HAD BEEN focused almost single-mindedly on al-Qaeda, Osama bin Laden, and international terrorism. Nobody in our shop had even considered shifting to Iraq. Now, we had to turn on a dime and redirect our attention. We quickly learned that much of the pressure to go to war in Iraq was coming from two sources—the Office of the Vice President (OVP) and the Office of the Secretary of Defense (OSD). In other words, Dick Cheney, Donald Rumsfeld, and their subordinates. The key players below them included several people in the OVP, including Lewis "Scooter" Libby, Cheney's chief of staff, and David Addington, his legal counsel; at OSD, the cast of characters below Rumsfeld was led by Deputy Secretary of Defense Paul Wolfowitz and Undersecretary of Defense Douglas Feith.

As best we could tell, the Joint Chiefs of Staff and their two- and three-star subordinates were less than enthusiastic about an Iraq invasion. The generals and admirals could make their best case for caution, but they were in a position of weakness. If the suits, reflecting the commander-in-chief's will, said the United States was going to war, the uniforms would salute and follow orders. Under our Constitution, there was only one other choice: Resign your commission in protest. To the best of my knowledge, none did.

Cheney, Rumsfeld, and their people put great stock in what they were hearing from the Iraqi National Congress (INC), a group of Iraqi exiles generally based in London. In particular, they looked to Ahmed Chalabi, the INC's leader. Chalabi was a real piece of work. He was an Iraqi Shiite whose family left the country in 1956 when he was twelve years old. He lived abroad, mainly in England and the United States, got a Ph.D. in mathematics from the University of Chicago, became a banker, made a lot of money, and got in trouble with the Jordanian government over alleged financial fraud. Through the INC, and on his own, Chalabi had been feeding his Washington friends in high places a steady diet of dirt on the Iraqi dictator and his plans. Saddam had weapons of mass destruction. He intended to use them. He had close ties to al-Qaeda and even to bin Laden himself.

As I said before, our intelligence suggested that Saddam did have weapons of mass destruction, certainly chemical and biological weapons and a nuclear program in development; in our view, that's why he wouldn't permit international weapons inspectors, whom he had expelled in 1998, to return to Iraq. But the rest of Chalabi's sales pitch was complete bullshit. There was no evidence to suggest Saddam was intending to use these weapons or that he even had the delivery systems to do so. The Osama-Saddam connection was partly notional: After all, didn't both men despise the United States? But it also turned on an alleged meeting in Prague in early April 2001 between Mohammed Atta and an Iraqi intelligence officer. Atta was one of the key hijackers of American Airlines Flight 11 on September 11, 2001. Ergo, Saddam must have had something to do with 9/11, perhaps even with the planning of it.

The Atta tale of a meeting in Prague, promoted heavily by Vice President Cheney, proved to be untrue. And on the general proposition of an unholy alliance between Iraq and al-Qaeda, there was a large troubling fact that had to be ignored: Osama bin Laden reviled Saddam Hussein as much as he did the United States. There's that old saw about the enemy of my enemy being my friend, which

I suppose encouraged some true believers to buy into the idea of an Osama-Saddam alliance. But at the agency, the alleged partnership between this odious pair was widely known as the Big Lie.

At that point, in 2002, Chalabi was no stranger to me, although I'd never met the man. While I was still an analyst, the agency received a request from one of the congressional oversight committees on Capitol Hill seeking detailed information on Chalabi. The reason, unstated, was almost certainly because Chalabi was continuing to cultivate friends in high places, and committee members wanted to know if he was on the level. I had been following Chalabi for much of my professional life, so I was enlisted to draft the CIA response. I wanted to be especially thorough. There's an old joke at the agency that you can anger your boss and live to tell the tale, but never run afoul of the security, finance, or medical departments of the CIA because they can end your career. A corollary: While the CIA works for the president, you never want to run afoul of Congress because it can really do you damage.

Working with two junior analysts, I researched and wrote a long response to the committee's questions, sourced the document, and sent it through the agency's long coordination and review process. In the Directorate of Intelligence, everybody with a stake in what is said in such papers gets a shot at them. On this one, everybody in the building agreed with what I was saying—that Ahmed Chalabi was completely unreliable, a serial fabricator who should be avoided at all costs. We sent the paper to the State Department for comments. What we got back was our document with every critical point deleted; what remained was only his personal information. Stunned and outraged, I called the analyst—someone I respected enormously—at State's Bureau of Intelligence and Research. She chuckled at my initial reaction and then turned serious. She had nothing to do with the changes, she insisted. It had been a policy decision, made far above our pay grades.

I consulted a colleague about what to do next. We were

mystified; State's Near East experts knew Chalabi well—well enough to know he was a con man. We were confident about what I had written, and we could ignore State in responding to Congress if we saw fit. Which is what we did: We sent my original paper, the one vetted by my CIA colleagues, to the committee, putting us on record. Ahmed Chalabi richly deserved the figurative scarlet letter: an order that no agency officer was to have contact with him.

Still, no-contact order or not, the willing suspension of disbelief seemed to be epidemic in certain Bush administration quarters during those days. In the vice president's office and at Defense, they were just lapping up Chalabi's stuff. The question was why. These guys weren't stupid. Yes, we knew ideology played a big part: They thought they could remake the Middle East, and toppling Saddam was central to the effort. They really did think our troops would be greeted as liberators in Baghdad and everywhere else in Iraq. I attended meetings on Iraq nearly every day, often by teleconference, and heard one NSC official actually say the words: "They're going to throw flowers at us on the streets of Baghdad." Who knows, it might have worked out that way if the administration had used the plan envisioned by some experts after the regime was toppled in April 2003. That plan, and it had several permutations, would have saturated Iraq with an occupation force of at least three hundred thousand soldiers, marines, and allied troops; the idea was to secure critical infrastructure, win hearts and minds with a benign, overwhelming presence, get Iraq back on its feet, nurture political pluralism, and leave as quickly as events would permit.

But as numerous books in recent years have pointed out, the administration completely botched the critical months after President Bush announced an end to major combat operations. The answer to why we're still in Iraq to this day has almost everything to do with the failures of leadership in 2003 and 2004 and, in some cases, the ascendance of rank deception—deliberate distortions of the facts on the ground.

It's also important to concede that we probably dropped the ball on our reading of Saddam and what he would do. In many respects, during the period leading up to the beginning of the war, Saddam seemed to be goading us to invade. Why would he do that if he didn't actually have weapons of mass destruction? In retrospect, I believe it's because we didn't understand the importance of "face" in Arab culture. Saddam couldn't act in ways that made him look weak among his Arab neighbors and especially to his own people. There were no chemical, biological, or nuclear weapons, but he couldn't simply go public and say, "All right, all right, I give up. In fact, I destroyed all those programs. Come in and see for yourselves. And, by the way, would you please lift the sanctions now?"

Conversely, Saddam wasn't very smart in his reading of the American side. He didn't understand that an American president generally means what he says when he threatens war. He probably thought Bush was posturing by sending troops to Kuwait and two carrier groups to the Gulf; by negotiating with the Turks, Jordanians, and Syrians for overflight clearance; and by going to the United Nations for a new resolution. In Saddam's world, this was all part of the game—what he expected from us because we had to *look* tough even when we'd finally come to some accommodation and let him lose with dignity. He probably calculated that our spies would be able to learn, without admitting inspectors, that his programs were history and that we'd eventually back away rather than risk a real shooting war.

What our spies and informants were noticing, of course, was that Iraqi scientists specializing in chemistry, biology, and, to a lesser extent, nuclear power kept showing up at international symposia. They presented papers, listened to the presentation of others, took copious notes, and returned to Jordan, where they could transit overland back to Iraq. We also saw Iraq's embassy in Amman, Jordan, used as an active agent to circumvent sanctions. Throughout the 1990s, Iraq had an aggressive program to buy "dual use" products—that is, components and subcomponents that could be used for both civilian and military purposes.

Chalabi's "intelligence," meanwhile, kept worming its way into our collective work product, even though our no-contact order meant that he was persona non grata to the CIA. He managed this because he fed material to his civilian friends at the Pentagon, who then put it into the larger pool of intelligence as DODIR, or Department of Defense Intelligence Reporting. DODIR tends to be, at best, spotty in its reliability, since any Defense Department official, in a suit or a uniform, can collect information and write it up as a military intelligence report. We would often see reports that were largely cut-and-paste jobs of newspaper articles classified as "confidential" and sent along as intelligence. The attribution needed only to be "a reliable source." Some of these reports became very detailed on Iraq's WMD programs and on the purchase of component parts for those programs. But there was no specific sourcing. The sources were Chalabi and his underlings.

Was it an intelligence failure? Yes. Bad information was getting into our intelligence system. Was it a failure of analysis? No. The agency's protocols for analyzing the quality of information are very detailed. Although I cannot discuss the specifics, suffice it to say that the CIA does a credible job of distinguishing between untested sources and genuinely reliable sources. There was no way for us to prevent the corruption of DOD intelligence when Chalabi's recipients were drooling over his awesome sources and insisting that we take what they were saying with utmost seriousness. We simply were not permitted to vet these "reliable" sources.

Secretary of State Colin Powell raised some red flags about Chalabi and questioned the stuff he was funneling into the intelligence mix. But he got outmaneuvered by Vice President Cheney at every turn. Cheney managed to run circles around everyone, including my boss, George Tenet, and even the president of the United States.

On Sunday, January 26, 2003, I had just returned from a

weekend visiting Chris and Costa at my folks' house in Pennsylvania; in those days, my routine was to leave Pennsylvania in the late afternoon; when I hit the D.C. area, I'd head straight for the office, arriving around 10 p.m. to read cables. I'd then go home for a few hours, then return at 4 or 5 a.m. Monday. The objective was to clear my in-box, or at least reduce the size of the stack in it, so I wouldn't be overwhelmed when the regular workday began later Monday morning. That evening, Bob Grenier was still at the office; at a conference table near him was a familiar face in unfamiliar clothes—Colin Powell, in jeans and a T-shirt.

"What's he doing here tonight?" I had no idea what was going on.

"Oh, he's going over the latest draft of the State of the Union," Bob said. "We're in a battle over the line about the yellowcake." I shrugged and went about my business.

This particular battle dated back to the previous fall, when President Bush was preparing to deliver a national security address in Cincinnati. His draft included language suggesting that Saddam had sought "yellowcake," a mix of uranium oxides, in Niger, a country in northwest Africa. The context was that the Iraqi dictator wanted the stuff to help him develop his nuclear weapons program. As the draft circulated among the various agencies and departments on the review list, we got involved in a game of ping-pong with the White House. Director Tenet, relying on agency analysts, insisted that the yellowcake line could not be supported by intelligence and needed to go. In the back-and-forth, Tenet finally prevailed and Bush gave the speech in Cincinnati on October 7, 2002, with no mention of Niger, Africa, or yellowcake.

Now, our people and Secretary Powell, probably the most admired person in the Bush administration, were trying to keep the genie in the bottle once again. We had seen the original report, which contained misspellings, multiple fonts, and other indications that it was a forgery. With Powell's support, we managed to purge the language from the State of the Union address, or so we thought.

But on Tuesday night, January 28, 2003, George Bush delivered an address that included the following sixteen words: "The British government has learned that Saddam Hussein recently sought significant quantities of uranium from Africa." Between Sunday night and Tuesday night, someone had overruled the CIA and the secretary of state and, presumably, the National Security Council staff to reinsert the suspect line. The someone, the world would later learn, was Vice President Dick Cheney.

Director Tenet would not tender his resignation until July 2004. By then, he had become a party to Colin Powell's presentation to the UN Security Council on February 5, 2003, making the case for the existence of Iraqi weapons of mass destruction—a spectacle of flimsy evidence supported by visual props, including the director of central intelligence seated prominently behind the secretary of state. Tenet would have his integrity sullied and his judgment called into question. The words "slam dunk" would attach to him in a pejorative context that had nothing to do with basketball and everything to do with politics as a contact sport. But if there was a beginning to the end of Tenet as DCI, it was probably Bush's 2003 State of the Union address.

Tenet deserved better. He was director during one of the most tumultuous times in CIA history, and he made plenty of mistakes. Who doesn't? But the sharp criticism of him, in isolation from the White House he served, strikes me as unfair. He did the best he could, for the most part, trying to be an honest broker for the intelligence community in an executive branch with more hidden agendas than even Richard Nixon could have dreamed up. He wanted—perhaps too much—to please.

16

□ □ □

I FIRST SAW George Tenet up close in the early 1990s when JoAnne and I attended the Greek Orthodox Church of Saint George in Bethesda, Maryland, where the parents of Tenet's wife, Stephanie, were regulars. At the time, he was director for intelligence programs at the National Security Council, so every once in a while, the priest would make a comment about how honored we were to have such a distinguished man in our congregation. I made a mental note: This guy's in the White House and involved in intel, so he must be pretty important.

He came to the CIA in July 1995 as deputy director of central intelligence, the DDCI in the world of intel alphabets. I confess that the idea of a fellow Greek near the top of the pyramid was appealing. We Greeks are a clannish bunch, I suppose; we stick together and try to help one another. How could having Tenet near the top possibly hurt?

Still, the CIA is a massive organization, with thousands of employees. It wasn't until the summer of 1997 that I first met him, shortly after he took over the top job. He was standing in the shish kebab line behind my brother, Emanuel, and me at the Saint George Greek Food Festival. I was saying that I thought the best *loukoumades,* or Greek doughnuts with honey and cinnamon on them, were made on the island of Chios. The voice behind me piped up: "Me, too! Chios definitely has the best *loukoumades.*" I turned and stared into the face of George Tenet. *Okay, junior, there's no better time to meet the boss than right now. Think of something clever. Or witty or wise.*

"Oh, hello, Mr. Tenet. I'm one of your analysts, John Kiriakou. Nice to meet you," I said, extending my hand. Well, *that* was bright, I thought.

"Oh, nice meeting you," he said, shaking hands. We chatted for a minute and went our separate ways.

A month later, he was doing a walk around our office, trying to introduce himself to all the analysts.

As he approached my desk, he registered recognition and said he remembered me. I wanted to make sure he remembered the name as well as the face.

"Yes, sir, nice to see you again," I said. "John Kiriakou, nice to see you."

He became director of central intelligence in July 1997. About eight months later, I was called in to brief him and his deputy, John McLaughlin, on Iraq. It was a Sunday, so I put on my good suit and met my office director at Langley before we went up to the DCI's suite. Tenet's secretary ushered us in. McLaughlin, a gem of a guy, was impeccably dressed in a suit that put my Sunday best to shame. Tenet, however, was treating the day as casual Sunday in the extreme; he was wearing jeans torn at one knee and a red-and-black plaid shirt, the kind lumberjacks wear. He's a stocky guy so he looked a little like the picture-book image of Paul Bunyan.

After the briefing, he took me aside and asked, "So where are your people from?" This is standard operating procedure when Greeks meet: As I said, we're a clannish tribe, and everyone figures they must have people in common.

"All four of my grandparents came from Rhodes."

"Ohhhh," he said, drawing it out, "an islander. You islanders think you're better than the mainlanders."

"Oh, no, sir, not at all." This islander-versus-mainlander business is a long-standing competition among Greeks, signifying absolutely nothing. "Where are your people from?"

"Mine are from Epirus," he said. That's in the northwestern corner of Greece, but the part where his family came from is now in Albania. We exchanged a few more words on the lands of our antecedents' birth, then went home to separate Sunday dinners.

A couple of months later, I was supposed to join a handful of other analysts in briefing the director on several issues. The minute he spotted me, Tenet was at it again. "Kiriakou, tell me one more time, where are your people from?"

"We're from Rhodes."

"Riiight," he said, drawing out the word again. "You islanders, you all think you're better than us mainlanders, don't you?"

"No, sir, we don't think we're better at all." *An inside joke with the DCI? I suppose there are worse things that could connect us. But maybe I should be careful. I'm not sure what's happening here.*

After my temporary assignment in Europe, I was back at headquarters walking down the hall one day with Katherine, whom I had begun to date, and there he was, coming from the opposite direction. As usual, Tenet was chomping on the unlit cigar that usually occupied one or the other corner of his mouth all day long. Our eyes made contact and I said, "Hello, sir, how are you?"

"How are you, islander? Still think you're better than I am?"

Here we go again. "No, sir, I've never thought that I'm better than you are." And so it went for another two or three rounds of imagined Greek rivalry before he walked on.

Katherine was mystified: "What was that all about?"

"I don't know. The first couple of times he said it, I thought he was kidding, that it was a joke between us, kind of funny. But now? I have no idea what he's thinking."

In the spring of 2002, I briefed him again, this time after I'd captured Abu Zubaydah. Tenet has a gruff, in-your-face kind of style, very personal. I don't know what I expected. I would have happily settled for an "attaboy" with an accompanying chuck to the shoulder.

Instead, he turned to one of the other people in the room and said, "Islander. He thinks he's better than I am."

I went through my ritual denials: Believe me, I didn't think I was better than he was.

"You islanders all think you're better than the mainlanders," he went on. "Why? Because you guys were fishing while we were up in the mountains?" Now it's fishing versus mountain shepherds? What the hell does that mean?

Afterward, as we walked out, Bob Grenier asked me whether I had some kind of beef with the director.

"Bob, I swear to God, I don't even know how this began, but he does it every time I see him."

During the Iraq war, he did it on a Saturday morning in front of two or three dozen people. And then, shortly before I left the agency, we met again. After we exchanged hellos and how-are-yous, he went at it:

"Have you done anything to adjust that attitude of yours?" I threw up my hands and made my case for islander-mainlander equality one last time. I haven't seen or talked to him since.

Is there a point to this story of intra-Greek fencing? I think so. In the CIA's earliest days, during the late forties, fifties, and early sixties, its personnel profile tended to be white Anglo-Saxon Protestant, Ivy League or exclusive small college, and moneyed. That started to change in subsequent decades, as the agency began to compete against other government and private-sector employers and broaden its recruiting to include women, African Americans, and even white ethnics with strange names like Kiriakou.

But the image of the CIA as a place for privileged types with impeccable pedigrees has lingered on. There's a joke at the agency that one day we're all going to wake up and the American people are going to be on to us, recognizing that we aren't quite worthy compared with the people who preceded us.

My hunch is that George Tenet went through the same emotional insecurity. Here was a guy who grew up in New York—Queens, not Manhattan—and whose father was an immigrant running a diner. You can achieve anything in America, we were told by our parents and grandparents from the old country, and Tenet certainly over-achieved. He went to fine schools—Georgetown University for his undergraduate degree and Columbia University for his master's—and he became the DCI at the relatively young age of forty-four. After a period of musical chairs at the top, with three directors in barely five years, Tenet did wonders for morale. He often had lunch in the cafeteria so people could see him, and he used those times to walk around and shake hands. He promoted a lot of people, many who deserved it, some who did not. He worked long and hard and, when he was kept on by President Bush, it looked like he had tenure, or at least as close to it as a political appointee can get.

But I sensed that he thought of himself as an outsider and even a pretender, not quite up to the job—a feeling echoed by agency people who knew him far better than I did. Tenet did want to please his bosses. No surprise there: In that respect, he was like the rest of us. But I felt, and so did others at the CIA, that he may have taken it too far and become too reluctant to talk truth to power at the highest level—that is, to the president of the United States. The business with enhanced interrogation techniques was an example of what I mean. In the post-9/11 frenzy, it's fairly clear that many in the White House, especially those in Vice President Cheney's orbit, wanted to do whatever it took to extract information from our high-profile detainees. Tenet could have raised cautionary flags about the use of—let's be charitable here—suspect techniques. In-stead, he seemed to play cheerleader to an audience eager to em-brace them.

The islander-versus-mainlander banter seemed to be, and was, harmless on its face. But it was clearly something that tapped into Tenet's sense of self, perhaps reflecting a perception that others looked down on him for reasons beyond his control. It wasn't true, so far as I knew, but maybe there was no persuading the director's subconscious mind of that.

THE MEN AND women of the Central Intelligence Agency, at least during my fourteen-plus years in its employ, were typical of many organizations—a mixed bag, but with many more talented people than the agency's fiercest critics would have Americans believe. On the key point, they coalesced as one. Rarely in my time at CIA did I encounter anyone who wasn't dedicated to the mission of gathering information, analyzing it, and presenting it to policy makers, who use it to further the interests of U.S. national security. As best as I could tell—no one took a poll—the agency included Republicans, Democrats, and independents in roughly equal numbers. But the "product," the analysis presented to the executive and legislative branches of government, was strictly nonpartisan. And the quality of that analysis, for the most part, was quite high.

Good analysts generally color their work because it's almost impossible to make a case for a conclusion with 100 percent certainty. The world of intelligence gathering and analysis isn't black-and-white. Still, the shades of gray can become disconcerting and obscure the central argument. Too often, senior people force caveats into analysis simply to protect the agency against being wrong. That, in turn, can make it a lot easier for people elsewhere—say, in the White House—to cherry-pick analysis and extract from it what they want to support a specific policy decision.

Risk aversion, in fact, is an occupational hazard at the CIA. Part of the problem can be traced to oversight, particularly congressional oversight of agency operations. The history of the CIA, at least over the past four decades, reflects a tendency to overcorrect—hitting the brakes when its congressional overseers believe the agency has become too aggressive, hitting the accelerator when more active measures are wanted. In the mid-1970s, after the Vietnam War and

Watergate, it was all brakes. After 9/11, they wanted us to hit the gas and go after the bad guys.

Fair enough: The CIA may not be a democracy, but it is the creature of one and it serves at the pleasure, and sometimes the whim, of those elected to their jobs as the people's representatives. But risk aversion can become a cultural trait, too, an inbred cover-your-ass instinct where even a reasonable venture risks getting rolled because someone up the line has a mindless twitch. Tenet's predecessor as DCI, John Deutch, for example, even implemented a new regulation establishing strict procedures for the recruitment and retention of any agent with known or suspected involvement in human rights violations or criminal activity. Each such case would require approval either by the agency's lawyers or by the director himself. Deutch was responding to a 1995 miniscandal in which the Guatemalan husband of an American citizen was murdered by a man with ties to the CIA. But the impact on the morale of case officers abroad was devastating, for obvious reasons.

Once, when I was in Athens, I wanted to enlist a guy who was a bona fide terrorist. We'd been in fairly regular contact, and I believed he had come around to trust me, at least to the point where he thought we could work together. I hadn't made the pitch yet, but since he was ready, I asked headquarters for permission to formally recruit him. If he agreed, we'd have an official relationship and, presumably, the agency would learn a great deal about the operations of his group.

Weeks passed, then a few months. When I asked what was up, I was told they were working on it. Finally, I got a message saying they were going to deny the request because agency attorneys were worried about us getting in bed with terrorists. The gist of the message was "If he's as bad as you say, we don't want to be working with him, or be seen working with him." The entire point was that he *was* a bad guy—someone who could help get us inside a terrorist group and perhaps save American lives.

It's strange how things sometimes turn out. In December 1999, Tenet hosted the annual Christmas party in the lobby of the original headquarters building; it was an opportunity to meet and greet, to shake the director's hand, and hear "good job" from him. One of my colleagues on Greek terrorism back at headquarters introduced himself to the boss and told him what he did at the agency. "Oh, Greek terrorism," Tenet said. "That's an issue that cuts very close to home. If there's anything I can do for you guys, let me know."

"As a matter of fact, sir..." After hearing my colleague's lament, Tenet summoned an assistant and told him to handle the problem. The next day, I got approval to recruit my agent. But should a clandestine operative have to count on dumb luck—a chance encounter at a Christmas party—to get an okay for a bold proactive step that could save American lives? I don't think so. Tenet, to his credit, didn't think so either. After 9/11, he effectively scrapped the regulation.

Fortunately, bureaucrats who seem to thrive on inhibiting innovation rather than encouraging it fill cubbyholes here and there at Langley, but they tend not to lead the place. Those at the top include some of the best of the best in our government. I want to mention just four of them.

STEVE KAPPES IS the CIA officer everyone wanted to be: a brilliant man, unfailingly gracious to colleagues, junior and senior, and with the highest ethnical standards to boot. I first met him overseas, when I was a junior analyst on loan to our ambassador to a Middle Eastern country because I knew a lot about the local personalities; Kappes didn't and needed to be briefed during his visit. I conducted my briefing for him and a few others and invited questions. The others were quiet, but Kappes was like a great investigative reporter, politely probing here, eliciting further information there, getting me to provide a more complete briefing. By the time we were done, I had learned two things: how to be a better briefer and a bit about how the mind of a truly impressive agency officer worked.

Kappes got caught up in a contretemps during the Bush years that showed what he was made of. After Tenet resigned, Bush named Porter Goss as his new CIA director. Goss, a congressman from Florida, had been a clandestine operative for the agency during the 1960s and, more recently, chairman of the House Permanent Select Committee on Intelligence. When he came to the CIA, he brought along some of his own people, including his chief of staff, Patrick Murray. One day, Murray reamed out Mike Sulick, who was associate deputy director for operations at the time, about another top employee's alleged leaking of classified information. Sulick was having none of it, and he and Murray got into a heated argument in Kappes's office. Sulick stormed out; Murray apparently told Kappes, then the deputy director for operations, that Sulick needed to be fired or transferred. Sulick, a stalwart at the CIA, had done nothing wrong, and Kappes knew it. Instead of firing or transferring him, Kappes resigned. So did Sulick. Then John McLaughlin, the deputy director of the CIA, did the same.

The loss of these three valuable men, for no good reason, was the beginning of the end for Porter Goss; he was gone early in 2006, replaced at CIA by air force general Michael Hayden. Hayden and his boss, John Negroponte, the new director of national intelligence, were wise enough to bring back both Kappes and Sulick, this time with Kappes as deputy CIA director and Sulick as deputy director for operations.

During Goss's troubled tenure, Bob Grenier, a top operations officer I have mentioned often, was also removed from his job as head of the Counterterrorist Center. With that, the CIA lost one of its finest and most effective leaders. Bob's true love was analysis, and he had originally sought positions in the Directorate of

Intelligence when the agency first hired him. He would have excelled there, too, because he is whip smart, unflappable, utterly honest, and nobody's yes-man. But he spent most of his career overseas, in operations I cannot discuss here. It wasn't just his colleagues in the clandestine service who counted on his intelligence and judgment. The U.S. ambassador to Pakistan once told me that she overruled her own State Department on more than one occasion based solely on Bob's wise counsel during his time there as senior officer in country.

His deep understanding of Afghanistan and its tribal culture paid off after the attacks of September 11, 2001. He was one of the chief planners who conceived the U.S. intelligence and military strategy of winning over Pashtun tribes in the south and working with the Northern Alliance to topple the Taliban. His work impressed President Bush. Enough so, said Bob Woodward in his book *Bush at War,* that the president asked Tenet to assign Bob to the agency's Iraq-related efforts. That's how he became the CIA's Iraq mission manager.

Another giant at the agency was Cofer Black, whom I've mentioned before. I don't want to give a false impression: Cofer and I were never close friends. He was my boss three levels up, and I respected him enormously. He was a legend at the agency for many reasons: his leadership skills, his ability to talk straight and colorfully, his capacity for clear thinking, and his instinct to act when others were reticent. He was also a legend because of his role in the capture of Ilich Ramírez Sánchez, aka Carlos the Jackal. In the 1970s, Carlos was one of the world's most notorious terrorists, working on behalf of various Palestinian groups and state sponsors of terrorism. If he wasn't the most wanted man on the planet, he certainly was on the short list. In the early 1990s, having moved around the Middle East and North Africa seeking safe haven, Carlos showed up in Khartoum, which turned out to be his undoing.

In 1994, Cofer Black was chief of the CIA's office in the Sudanese capital. At the same time, a longtime agency contract officer, Billy Waugh, was in country on business I cannot discuss here. Billy is a legendary figure in his own right, a former Army Special Forces noncommissioned officer who was awarded a Silver Star, four Bronze Stars, and eight Purple Hearts, mainly for his service in Vietnam.

One day, Billy happened to be walking through a Khartoum vegetable market when he spotted a guy he thought was Carlos himself; the man, a Caucasian, stood out in the sea of Sudanese faces. He rushed back to the office and found Cofer getting some exercise on a treadmill. As Billy tells the story:

"Cofer, I know this is going to sound crazy, but I just saw Carlos the Jackal in the vegetable market." Cofer laughed so hard he almost fell off the treadmill.

"Billy, give me a break. What do you want me to do, call in an air strike or something just because you think you saw Carlos?"

"I'm serious, it's Carlos the Jackal. I'm sure of it."

"All right," Cofer said, "get a team together and get me a photo."

Billy put a team together and they visited the vegetable market every day for a month. No Carlos. Everyone was thinking, well, maybe old Billy—he was then in his mid-sixties—is having trouble with his eyesight; it happens. Finally, just when they were about to give up, Carlos went vegetable shopping again. On the spot, the team devised a plan. Two of Billy's guys pretended to have a fight, pushing and shoving and maybe even landing a few blows. Naturally, they drew a crowd, which formed a big circle around Billy's two actors pretending to duke it out in the middle of Khartoum. Carlos dashed over to take a look; as he was craning his neck in an effort to glimpse the action, Billy was able to snap off a roll of film. Even Cofer thought the guy was the real deal: If it wasn't Carlos, it was the doppelgänger who retired the trophy.

Cofer informed headquarters while Billy put a tail on Carlos so our guys could figure out where he lived. We didn't have a warrant out for him, but France wanted him for murder for three car bombings in Paris.

With the help of Sudanese authorities, Carlos was seized, drugged, and handed off to French officials. In Paris, he was convicted and sentenced to life in prison in late 1997. By that time, Cofer Black's star was rising fast at the CIA, ascendant in part because of his involvement in the capture of this notorious terrorist.

Cofer Black didn't need to surround himself with buddies, and he didn't need to be the smartest guy in the room. He brought together the best operations officers in the building during his time as head of CTC—people who had worked all over the world and knew what to do after 9/11 when Cofer and others set their sights on Afghanistan. One of them was the indomitable Billy Waugh, who was still a contract employee, or "Greenbadger," at the agency. I ran into him in the hall at headquarters in early January 2002, just short of his seventy-second birthday.

"Billy, you still around?"

"Yeah, I've been in Afghanistan."

"What were you doing in Afghanistan?"

"Blowing up bridges, but don't tell anybody," he said with a grin. I didn't know whether to believe him. I later learned that he'd gone in with Gary Schroen's heroic team to aid the Northern Alliance and help crush the Taliban.

During that period, Jim Pavitt was deputy director for operations. Another major figure in one of the agency's most troubled times, Pavitt was smart, accomplished, and highly respected. I can't be sure, but my hunch is that the attacks of 9/11 were a burden that weighed heavily on him, as it probably did on many other top people at the agency. During the buildup to the invasion of Iraq, there were regular briefings in his office. As Bob Grenier's executive assistant, I was the junior officer and briefer among the heavyweights, which meant, among other things, that I got the most uncomfortable chair. It happened to be situated at one of the front corners of Pavitt's big desk, perfectly positioned for its occupant to see a letter perched on an acrylic stand. The letter was always there, clearly a piece of paper that Pavitt valued. I was able to read most of it—anyone sitting on that chair could have done so. It was from Mike Scheuer, a prominent participant in the Osama bin Laden unit that the agency had set up to target and ideally seize or kill the world's top terrorist.

Since leaving the CIA, Scheuer has been a serious critic of Bush administration policy and of the agency's timidity when it came to pulling the trigger on bin Laden. The letter began: "Dear Jim, I think you suck." That was the diplomatic part: The rest of his critique of Pavitt was laced with language that might impress the screenwriters for any number of HBO dramatic series.

On the last day I was briefing, I had a small moment alone with Pavitt and couldn't help myself: "Sir, do you mind if I ask you, why do you have this letter from Mike Scheuer up there on your desk?"

He chuckled for a brief moment. "Because Mike Scheuer is the only person at this place who ever had the balls to talk to me like that. Seeing it every day keeps me grounded."

I thought that was an excellent answer.

A CHERISHED AXIOM at the CIA is that its successes necessarily remain shrouded in secrecy while its failures and embarrassments get ample attention from congressional overseers, book authors, investigative reporters, and others who simply detest the very idea of clandestine activity by a democratic government. What isn't much discussed in the ongoing debates and controversies over the agency's efficacy are the CIA's internal operating procedures and its corporate culture, if you will.

Others may decide to examine such matters at length. For the purposes of this book, let me make two observations based on my nearly fifteen years at the agency. First, the CIA is a remarkably insular organization, and not by accident. Other organizations may frown upon intimate relationships among colleagues. The CIA, without explicitly saying so in any policy manual, seems to encourage such relationships or, at a minimum, does nothing to discourage them. The reason makes perfect sense. Agency officers work awful hours—long, irregular, at night, and on weekends. Unlike the vast majority of employees in the public or private sector, CIA people cannot discuss their assignments and daily labors with their spouses. The exception to the rule, of course, is when the husband or wife is also employed by the CIA. I'm cleared, she's cleared, we can bring the office home at night and talk about it.

My first marriage fell victim to the insider-outsider dilemma; my hunch is that it would have failed anyway, but my inability to discuss with JoAnne what I was doing on those odd-hour assignments certainly hastened the outcome. Our problem was magnified exponentially at the CIA. There are doubtless solid marriages between CIA and non-CIA spouses. But office affairs are commonplace, and the divorce rate at the agency has to be significantly higher than the national average. Once, on an overseas assignment, I was bemoaning the breakup of my first marriage, mainly because of the impact on my sons, Chris and Costa, when one of the other three officers in the room started laughing. In a moment, three CIA men were comparing notes about marriages made and marriages ended. When the last guy finally rested, it added up to quite a tally: Three alpha males had recorded fourteen marriages among them.

My other observation derives in part from the first. With so many office affairs, it's inevitable that advancement within the organization does not always seem earned by the quality of the work. The CIA ought to be a meritocracy, certainly among its people who are not political appointees. When that system breaks down, morale suffers and every promotion is somehow suspect.

The CIA is a place where office politics is played with a vengeance, where duck and cover can become a smart career move, and where who you know can trump what you know and drive a career well beyond its level of competence. Think of it as the Peter Principle gone berserk.

17

□ □ □

IN SEPTEMBER 2000, when I reported to Langley after my home leave in New York, I was like Joe Btfsplk—the *Li'l Abner* character who always walked around with a dark cloud over his head. The biggest beef against me was the fistfight in Athens that almost got me booted out of the agency. That criticism was well deserved. We were trained to keep our cool in all situations, even under personal stress, and I'd simply lost it.

But in some agency quarters, the rap went beyond my dustup with the baker. The top CIA official for Europe at the time was reading the cable traffic, including reports of my pitching eastern European generals, breaking off side-view mirrors as part of a plan to pitch a Middle Eastern diplomat, and other assorted ploys that covert operatives improvise. Training cannot account for every situation, and the best of the bosses in the CIA encourage their case officers to exercise their creativity so long as they remain within the boundaries. That's what I was doing. But the European operations official, who had never served in the field as an operations officer, didn't see it that way. She argued that I had used a "heavy hand" and spread the word that I'd never work for her. Mary Margaret Graham was wrong: I did end up working for her—and it didn't turn out well.

My year as Bob Grenier's executive assistant, working fourteen- or fifteen-hour days, six days a week, was regarded by my superiors as a success. My reward was the flexibility to choose any position for which I was qualified by talent and civil-service grade. Jim Pavitt, then the deputy director for operations, threw out a bunch of possibilities: a deputy slot in a major European station or a senior position in a country where my fluency in Arabic would be a huge plus for our operations.

I was flattered by this display of confidence in me, but it wasn't what I wanted—or, more precisely, what I needed. The job with Bob had put a real strain on my ability to see my children every other weekend.

"They're young boys, and they need their father," I told Pavitt. "You know, what I'd really like is a domestic assignment." In addition to its headquarters in suburban Washington, D.C., the CIA has a substantial operation in another area of the United States where my background and talents could be put to good use as a case officer monitoring foreign nationals from South Asia, the Near East, and the Middle East.

"You know, that sort of assignment is not really career enhancing at all," Pavitt told me. "It's going to hold you back the whole time you're there as far as promotion is concerned."

I told him I understood, but in this case, family had to come first. Okay, he said, the domestic assignment it is.

Pavitt sent me to the region, over the vehement objections of our senior CIA officer there, one Mary Margaret Graham. The funny thing was, she was short of officers and had appealed to Langley for help. I happened to see the cable and sent her an e-mail saying that I would volunteer for whatever she needed me to do, because I wanted to contribute to our work in the area. I was headed her way, and I laid it on thick, hoping to get off on the right foot. In retrospect, I should have known better.

The trouble began almost immediately. On my first weekend, I attended a diplomatic function and met a colonel from a foreign country who was on assignment to an international organization I cannot name here. I asked him about his work.

He said he was involved in military research for a certain African country that I should not identify by name.

"No kidding," I responded. "Sounds very interesting." It did. In fact, Langley had sent a cable appealing for information on military research in that African country.

I took him out to dinner one night, and another time I had a barbecue and invited him over. In short order, we became fast friends. Meanwhile, I'd sent a cable to our office in the colonel's country, alerting them to the opportunity and the risk.

The opportunity was a chance to enhance our understanding of the African country's military programs. The risk was blowback from the colonel's superiors if they found out he was cooperating with us. I asked permission to go forward, and our office in the colonel's country, now apprised of the potential pluses and minuses, gave me the green light.

Things were moving well; I thought we'd come to a point where I could try to recruit him. I would drop my cover, tell him who I was, explain what I needed, and offer to put his children through college if that's what it took.

We were set to have dinner at a restaurant in midtown Manhattan; the reservation was for 7 p.m. At 4 p.m., I was wrapping up in the office, locking up my computer hard drive in the safe, and getting ready to do my surveillance detection route to the restaurant. My secure line rang. It was Mary Margaret, which was a shock because Mary Margaret never called me for any reason.

"I want you to stand down on this meeting tonight," she said.

"Are you kidding me? I'm going to recruit him tonight. I've been working on this for months."

"Stand down."

I didn't understand. "Well, did something come from headquarters?" I thought maybe the office in the colonel's home country had second thoughts and wanted the operation spiked.

"No," she said. "You're a GS-14. You should be recruiting hard targets like the Chinese, not wasting your time with low-hanging fruit." (GS, for General Schedule, is a grading system for federal employees, running from entry-level GS-1 to GS-15, the top level before moving up to the Senior Executive Service.)

"Mary Margaret, this is a headquarters requirement. They specifically said they need somebody to report on [this African country]."

"I'm telling you to stand down," she repeated. Then, without another word, she hung up the phone.

I canceled dinner, making some excuse. "No problem," he said. "We'll schedule it for another night." But there wouldn't be another night. I ducked his calls, not having the guts to break it off. Three months later, on New Year's Eve, I took his call. He wanted to wish me a happy new year. But he was a bit angry and certainly disappointed, saying that I turned out not to be the friend he thought I was. We had become buddies, in his mind and in my own, and my cutting him off so abruptly proved his point: I wasn't what he thought I was. The whole episode broke my heart.

ABOUT THE SAME time, my personal life was going through fresh turmoil. I had remarried on August 16, 2003, one of the happiest days of my life. But there was one bad omen: My parents couldn't attend because my dad had to have emergency back surgery the morning of the wedding day.

My divorce decree, meanwhile, said that either I or my representative had to pick up my children by 6 p.m. on those alternate Fridays or I'd lose the weekend. If I lost too many weekends, I risked losing joint custody. As I said before, my parents had been heroic in helping out, driving from New Castle to Warren, arriving before 6 p.m., then driving back. I'd dash to the airport, catch a plane to Pittsburgh, rent a car, and get to New Castle in time to tuck the kids into bed. It made for a very long day.

On November 18, 2003, my dad fell down the steps and hit his head—hard. They life-flighted him to Pittsburgh, but he died eight hours after the fall. My mother was so distraught by his sudden death that the stress aggravated a case of diabetic retinopathy, and she began to go blind. Needless to say, she couldn't drive anymore.

I took two weeks of leave to settle my dad's estate, to get his finances in shape, and, of course, to do my best to console my mom. I also made arrangements with my cousin Maria, who lived nearby in New Castle, to pick up my kids and get them to my folks' house. But I also needed at least a small change at the office, too. I didn't think it would be too much to ask, but I guess I forgot who'd have to sign off on the request.

When I returned to my new assignment in early December, Mary Margaret called and asked me to come to her office. She had the deputy chief with her, a spineless cipher who's now the chief, and she expressed her condolences. I thanked her and used the opportunity to ask her for a favor.

I explained the personal situation I now faced. Official hours were 9 a.m. to 5 p.m.

"Would it be possible," I asked, "if I worked eight to four every other Friday so I could get to my kids an hour earlier?"

She just stared at me, then said, "Well, eight to four isn't nine to five, is it?"

"Mary Margaret, I risk losing my kids here."

"You should have thought of that before you came here."

"Okay." I got up and left.

Later on, as I sat in my office with my head in my hands, a colleague wandered in.

"Rough day?" she asked.

Oh, yeah, I said, then replayed my little drama with Mary Margaret.

She asked whether I remembered an Alice Callahan, an analyst for the agency in the early nineties. Alice had left the CIA and was now working for a big accounting and consulting firm. Apparently, the firm had a group that did risk analysis and competitive intelligence and had been hiring people with our skills.

I gave Alice a call; she reported that her firm had an opening in its McLean, Virginia, office and that I should fax my résumé to her.

I did just that, but before sending it off, I vetted every single word and entry against a booklet the CIA's career center made available; the booklet said exactly what a CIA employee could say in a résumé without violating the agency's secrecy rules.

The interview process was familiar: There were a lot of psychological tests that posed ethical dilemmas. One that I found particularly interesting was this: Did you ever consciously violate the rules and not regret it?

My answer, I told my interviewer, would have to be yes. She asked about the context.

"I worked with a guy who had a series of security violations," I said. "He'd forget to spin the dial on the lock on his safe. Or he'd forget to put some classified paper in the safe. Well, the room was vaulted and alarmed, so nobody was going to wander in off the street and say, 'Oh, look at this classified document on trade secrets' or something like that."

The chief warned him: One more time and you're out and on the next plane to headquarters. Sure enough, I walked into the vault one morning and saw a classified document on his desk. So I shredded it. Am I sorry I did that? Not really. I knew it hadn't been compromised. But did I violate the rules? Yes, clearly, I did.

I won't belabor the back-and-forth with the firm. They offered me a job, and I accepted. I really had no other alternative. Mary Margaret had made it clear that she didn't give a fig about my dedication to the CIA and my belief in its mission, my years of award-winning service, or my desire to continue a career in an organization that had become an emotional, as well as professional, part of my life. She was demanding that I make a choice between my second family and my first family. Ask any committed parent: That's not a choice at all.

Still, my journey with Mary Margaret was far from over. It was like being pecked to death by ducks.

When I told her I would be leaving and where I was going, she asked whether I'd sought the job.

"No, they sought me," I said. The truth was, it was a mutual courtship. But it was none of her business how I came to the job.

She asked whether I'd had my résumé cleared. I told her I didn't write a résumé. Okay, that was a lie, but I'd had enough. At that point, I figured I owed that woman nothing.

"Oh, so you're saying they just decided they had to have John Kiriakou and came and got you?"

"That's exactly what I'm saying."

She dropped it, but we weren't done.

One of Mary Margaret's underlings came to me on my penultimate day on the job and apologetically explained what his boss wanted done.

"Look, she told me to whack you on your PAR." PAR was the acronym for Performance Appraisal Report. "It's a parting shot. It'll have my signature on it, but it doesn't come from me. I'm being ordered to do this."

This pathetic guy was covering his ass. He said more than once that he knew I had *wasta*. He'd had one Middle East tour, but he didn't speak Arabic. He did know an Arabic word for influence, though, and he was right: I did have some friends in high places at headquarters, and I suppose that added up to *wasta*.

"You do whatever you have to do," I told him. "But when you call her back, and I know you will, you tell her that I have documented absolutely everything that has happened to me here since the day I arrived. And you tell her, I don't care how important she is, I am not afraid of her."

Five minutes later, my secure phone rang.

"Hello, John."

"Hello, Mary Margaret."

"Can you come up to the office?"

"Certainly, Mary Margaret."

I called Katherine and filled her in. She was nervous: "Oh, my God, don't lose your temper. Don't lose your temper with her." But it was probably too late for that advice. Not every situation lights my short fuse, as Katherine certainly knew. But she also knew my history with the agency and about the fight with the Greek baker, among other episodes. This was one of those times, she figured, when I'd find it difficult to remain cool and collected.

Mary Margaret's secretary greeted me, told me to go in, and wished me good luck.

Mary Margaret wasn't alone. She had a top operations officer with her—a tame witness, I figured, and said as much to him. He didn't say a word.

She started calmly: "I understand you had quite an emotional outburst this morning."

I laughed. "Oh, Mary Margaret, no, no, no, I didn't have an emotional outburst. When I have an emotional outburst, people are going to read about it on the front page of *The New York Times*. That's an emotional outburst."

"And you're not afraid of me." It wasn't a question.

"Indeed, I'm not."

"Well, I think we should lay our cards on the table," Mary Margaret said. "I want to know what you have in this so-called file of yours."

"Mary Margaret, tomorrow is my last day. All I ask of you is to write a PAR that accurately reflects my performance here."

"I'm asking you a direct question," she said. "What do you have in this file?"

"And I'm telling you I don't think what I have in my file is relevant unless I don't get a PAR that accurately reflects my performance here."

Now, her tone wasn't so calm: "Let's just cut the bullshit. I'm going to write exactly what I think of you."

"And then I'm going to write exactly what I *know* of you. But what I write is going to go to the committees and to *The Washington Post*. And then you can deal with the fallout."

It was like I'd jabbed her with a Taser. She was visibly twitchy.

"All right, Mr. Tough Guy, I think you're full of shit."

She had finally lit the short fuse. "Okay, here's what I have," I said. "I work in an atmosphere that encourages sexual harassment."

"What? Are you kidding me?"

"I work in a group with three women, and I have a branch chief who is your protégé and who feels completely free to use the word 'cunt' in our branch meetings—to the point where the secretary covers her ears and pleads with him not to use it again. People can't use a single sentence without the word 'fuck' in it. I've never worked in an environment like this, and it's the kind of environment you've created."

"That's nonsense," she said. "I would never encourage an environment like that."

"Oh, really? And what about the Asian I was developing? When you told my branch chief to tell me to take the Asian guy to a strip club, spend two thousand dollars, and get blow jobs for the both of us at the end of the night?

"And what would the committee think if I'm spending two thousand dollars not just at a strip club, but a strip club owned by a big-time crime family? That's where you tell us to take our developmentals? To a mobbed-up strip club? To spend taxpayer money?"

It was like I'd punched her in the stomach. Her voice went quiet.

"Can you give me five minutes, please?"

I got up and walked out. The secretary had a big grin on her face.

"How's it going in there?"

"In the beginning, not so well," I said. "But I think I've got her on the run." People had begun to gather. Apparently, our voices had carried. Oh, hell, we'd been screaming at each other.

"We're pulling for you," the secretary said.

The secretary's phone was lit up; Mary Margaret had obviously called someone at headquarters. Five minutes turned into fifteen or twenty. Then she opened the door and asked me to come in. I sat in the same chair.

She got right to it. "What exactly do you want?"

"I'll repeat myself," and I did. "I'm not asking for any favors."

"I want you to promise me, in front of him"—she pointed at the Ops chief—"that what was said in this room is going to stay in this room."

"I want to read my PAR first."

Later that day, they wrote a PAR that did accurately reflect my performance during my six months under Mary Margaret's thumb. And I never said anything to the intelligence committees in Congress or to *The Washington Post*. Much later, I learned that Mary Margaret had sent a "burn notice" on me to the CIA director of personnel. In it, she apparently said I was a horrible person and a bad officer who should never be rehired if I ever tried to rejoin the agency. And she sent it the very day I left the CIA.

Mary Margaret Graham served one tour overseas in thirty years—and that one tour was not as an operations officer. After I left the agency, she rose to become the deputy director of national intelligence for collection—one of the top deputies to Director of National Intelligence Mike McConnell. She retired in early 2008.

Am I proud of how I behaved during my final days at the CIA? Hardly. I used words I rarely use, especially in mixed company, and I used bullyboy tactics when a more civil approach might have produced the same outcome. But I doubt it.

Consider my last conversation with Mary Margaret, a classic of sorts. "You have a big day tomorrow," she said in a saccharine sweet voice. "Packing and whatever it is you have to do. Why don't you just take the day off?" Maybe she was worried I'd do something to sabotage her. Who knows? I politely declined the offer.

"No, I insist, you take an admin day and we won't count it toward your vacation."

"I don't think so, thanks. There's always a chance someone might send a cable to headquarters and accuse me of time and attendance fraud. Count on me tomorrow."

So I went to the office and worked a normal day. I went to some meetings, I sat in on a seminar, I had coffee with a guy from Jordan.

I finished my day and turned in my badge. And then I went home.

EPILOGUE

YOU NEVER LEAVE the CIA, not really. You may resign in midcareer, as I did, or you may spend a working lifetime in its service before retirement and a gold watch, but the agency always remains a presence in your life. How could it not? The CIA, preferring to operate in government's invisible corridors, has become a lightning rod for unwanted attention over the six-plus decades since its founding. Its tightly wound culture both cements and fractures friendships, depending on the circumstances. It is a force that tugs at the sleeve of former employees, gently but insistently, even though you may have moved on.

In the late autumn of 2007, more than three years removed from agency employment, I hadn't been paying close attention to many of the issues then top of mind among intelligence professionals when I got a phone call from Richard Esposito, a reporter for ABC News. Years earlier, I had confirmed for Rich a story he had heard from a friend elsewhere in the federal government, and we had stayed in touch. Now he was calling about the story then dominating the headlines: The CIA had acknowledged that videotapes of harsh interrogations of some al-Qaeda prisoners had been destroyed even though agency and White House lawyers had urged that they be preserved. (Eighteen months later, the number of destroyed tapes was revealed; instead of a handful, as suspected earlier, some ninety-two tapes had been destroyed.) Rich's colleague, Brian Ross, ABC's chief investigative reporter, had asked him to ring me up because they had information that I might know something about what was on the tapes. If I did and if I was prepared to discuss it, he said, Ross wanted to interview me on camera.

I was equivocal, telling Esposito that I'd get back to him shortly with a firm answer. Katherine, my wife and the love of my life, is wise and cautious by nature, and her instincts were that I should politely decline this particular invitation. If you decide to do it, she added, you must be very careful about what you say. I knew what she meant. There was no way I could or would reveal classified information. But if I could help to clarify the issue, I felt the interview would be worth doing. I waited a couple of days, got back to Esposito, and told him I'd be happy to cooperate in any way I could so long as it did not involve classified information.

It wasn't my first brush with television that fall. In October, both ABC News and NBC News had interviewed me about an August trip I'd made to Afghanistan at the behest of Paramount Pictures, which had turned the giant best seller *The Kite Runner* into a film and now worried about the safety of its twelve-year-old Afghan stars. The film included a male rape scene, crucial to the story and muted on film, but still potentially inflammatory in Afghanistan's conservative social culture. My job was to see if Paramount's fears were justified; if they were, Paramount would take steps before the movie opened to evacuate the boys to a safe haven in the region, where they could be raised and educated until they reached adulthood. The concerns *were* justified, and in October, Richard Klein, a Middle East expert at McLarty Associates in Washington, flew to the United Arab Emirates to make the arrangements for the boys' new life.

The two networks sent camera crews to my house in suburban Virginia, filmed twenty minutes of an interview about my role in the film's off-screen ending, and cut the tape to twenty or thirty seconds of broadcast time on the evening news. I assumed ABC had pretty much the same thing in mind for the interview about the trashed interrogation tapes.

I assumed wrong. Brian Ross met me at ABC News's Washington studios on DeSales Street, sat me down, and interviewed me for forty-five minutes. When it was over, we exchanged a few pleasantries and shook hands, then Brian took off. A cameraman wandered over and volunteered that he thought the interview was "terrific," by which he meant that it was filled with news. "I wouldn't be surprised if they put it on the Web site because that was really interesting." Uh-oh, I thought. Had I gone too far?

The interview was supposed to be about the destroyed tapes, but Ross spent only the first two or three minutes on them before he segued to the issue of waterboarding and Abu Zubaydah. I probably should have demurred then and there, saying that these were subjects I didn't want to discuss publicly. Instead, I responded to Brian's questions.

President Bush had talked about the use of enhanced interrogation techniques on al-Qaeda prisoners, although he and others in the administration had never addressed the specifics. At that point, the torture memos were classified—off-limits to any current or former CIA officer inclined to go public. Still, Human Rights Watch and other nongovernmental organizations had been saying for more than two years that waterboarding was one of the enhanced techniques; if it was a secret that a few high-value al-Qaeda prisoners had been waterboarded, it was the worst-kept secret in Washington by December 2007. I honestly did not think that what I was saying was classified or even particularly sensitive, so I talked about Abu Zubaydah being waterboarded.

Waterboarding is torture, I told Ross, but it was legal and even justified, given the time and context of its use. People needed to understand the mind-set of the agency—indeed, the entire national-security apparatus of our government—in the months after 9/11. We were taken by surprise, and Osama bin Laden and his murderous sidekick, Ayman al-Zawahiri, were boasting of bigger strikes to come. We had to take them at their word and try to do everything humanly possible to forestall further attacks. Waterboarding and other enhanced interrogation techniques went through an elaborate review process—by attorneys for the National Security Council and the Justice Department, by Attorney General John Ashcroft, and by National Security Adviser Condoleezza Rice. There was nothing willy-nilly about it. Only after all these people had signed off on the techniques did the proposal go to the president for his signature. That was my take on it at that moment in late 2007, no more, no less.

I couldn't go into specifics, but I did tell Ross that what we learned from Abu Zubaydah probably had saved lives and disrupted attacks against American and allied interests. I also told him about my own experience—that I had been asked whether I wanted to be trained in these techniques, had sought guidance from a senior officer in the clandestine service, and had declined the training afterward based in part on the officer's wise and generous counsel.

On Monday morning, December 10, 2007, Brian Ross called to say that he and Esposito were going to put up a piece on ABC News's Web site, based on the interview, complete with video links to excerpts. That was what I expected based on what the ABC cameraman had suggested a couple days earlier. What I hadn't expected was what Ross said next: ABC News planned to run a three-minute segment on *World News with Charlie Gibson* that evening, followed by an eleven-minute clip on *Nightline* later on. The next day, *Good Morning America* would get its bite of the apple with a five-minute segment.

Ross invited me up to New York to watch *Nightline* go live. By the time I landed at LaGuardia Airport, *World News* had finished up and my cell phone had twenty-six voice mails, mostly from reporters at other networks seeking interviews. Someone—I could never track down the actual source amid all the denials—had given out my number, which apparently was being passed around like a joint at a college fraternity party. Okay, I thought, I'm committed to this now and had better see it through, for better or worse.

I returned as many of the calls as I could before crashing at my hotel, then started making the rounds the next morning. The *Today* show, 5 a.m. CNN *American Morning,* 6 a.m. CBS's *Early Show,* 7 a.m. Then it was midday news programs. At FOX, someone asked: Is it true you're a protégé of Ted Kennedy and you're running for Congress in Virginia? It was getting just that crazy.

One interviewer suggested I was guilty of hypocrisy: How could I reconcile my endorsement of waterboarding as legal and necessary under extraordinary circumstances and at the same time refuse to engage in it myself? A majority of Americans support the death penalty, I said, but I defy you to point out who in this studio would be willing to administer the lethal injection.

My position on waterboarding was nuanced, but television and talk radio were reducing it to black-and-white. Here we go again, I thought. After my Afghanistan run, I had coauthored an op-ed with Rich Klein of McLarty Associates. The piece, which ran in the *Los Angeles Times* and was picked up by eighty other papers, took issue with former defense secretary Donald Rumsfeld's assertion that Afghanistan was a peaceable kingdom with democracy taking firm root. In my experience, Kabul was an armed camp, and the situation there and throughout the country was deteriorating, not improving. Our piece drew fire from the talk-show terrorists, with Rush Limbaugh and Laura Ingraham, among others, labeling me an American-hating traitor for taking on Rumsfeld.

Now, these same people were calling me an American patriot because of my reluctant defense of waterboarding. On the left, opinion was divided. Some bloggers called me a hero for saying that waterboarding was torture; others were ready to string me up for torturing prisoners even though I hadn't participated in such acts. People just fixated on the sound bite that seemed to support their own view of the world. Before it was over, I got more than a dozen death threats. The local police were great about cruising our house every couple of hours, just to make sure there wasn't a can-do fanatic among the crank callers.

SINCE THEN, OF course, much has changed. We've tightened border security and airport security, and we have improved our counterterrorism capabilities. In the historic presidential campaign of 2008, the Republican nominee, Senator John McCain, the Democratic nominee, Senator Barack Obama, and his chief rival in the primaries, Senator Hillary Clinton, now our secretary of state, all labeled waterboarding as torture and rejected its use in the future. President Obama emphatically punctuated the point: He issued an executive order during his first days in office that limited all interrogations to the techniques used by the American military and detailed in the *U.S. Army Field Manual*. Then, in April 2009, the president declassified the memos on enhanced interrogation techniques and told CIA personnel that they would not be prosecuted for actions driven by the White House and Justice Department. That was a wise decision by our president.

Still, as of this writing, a prosecutor appointed by Attorney General Eric Holder is trying to determine whether CIA interrogations should be subject to a full criminal investigation. If the Justice Department decides to go ahead, it would effectively break President Obama's pledge to the CIA, since the Agency had legal cover, however dubious, to employ enhanced interrogation techniques. It would also be practically impossible for Justice Department lawyers to avert their eyes and ignore the people in the Bush Administration who seeded the legal ground for CIA interrogators.

Seven former CIA directors, serving Democratic and Republican presidents stretching back nearly four decades, have petitioned President Obama to reverse Holder's decision to press the case on CIA interrogations. They make the argument that a U.S. Attorney has already looked into allegations that Agency employees or contractors had exceeded their legal authority; in all cases save one, the U.S. Attorney declined to prosecute. "If criminal investigations closed by career prosecutors during one administration can so easily be reopened at the direction of political appointees in the next," they wrote, the decision not to prosecute would be rendered meaningless.

It's a fair point, as is their contention that cooperative efforts with the intelligence agencies of other countries would be jeopardized. I also agree with President Obama that his administration needs to look forward, not back. No one is above the law, but it probably would be difficult, if not impossible, to make a case against those claiming they gave the best legal advice they could, however flawed it turned out to be. I suspect the many reviews and Congressional inquiries of post-9/11 treatment of detainees will yield a relatively complete portrait that includes sins of omission as well as commission by the CIA and other government entities. Meanwhile, our country has huge problems at home and abroad that need the full attention of our leaders.

What I told Brian Ross in late 2007 was wrong on a couple of counts. I suggested that Abu Zubaydah had lasted only thirty or thirty-five seconds during his waterboarding before he begged his interrogators to stop; after that, I said he opened up and gave the agency actionable intelligence. I wasn't there when the interrogation took place; instead, I relied on what I'd heard and read inside the agency at the time. Now, we know that Abu Zubaydah was waterboarded eighty-three times in a single month, raising questions about how much useful information he actually supplied. In retrospect, it was a valuable lesson in how the CIA uses the arts of deception even among its own.

The national debate on waterboarding and other forms of torture got a second wind early in Obama's presidency, and I'm proud to have played a small part in it. In a larger sense, this is not an American conversation that has ended. If we have learned anything since 9/11, we have learned anew that a tension exists between protecting our national security and ensuring the human rights guaranteed in that most precious of documents, the U.S. Constitution. Our challenge, in a world of unprecedented threats, is to strike a balance between the polarities—to find that place where the two can live reasonably, if not comfortably, side by side.

It won't be easy. But then, it never was.

ACKNOWLEDGMENTS

FIRST, I WOULD like to thank Mike Ruby for the hundreds of hours he committed to helping me turn my ramblings into a coherent manuscript. Mike never lost his composure or sense of humor despite nine separate drafts I had to send through the CIA's notorious Publications Review Board. Thanks to Rich Klein, my dear friend, for getting the ball rolling in the first place and for his unflagging friendship and support through some dark days. Thanks to Flip Brophy at Sterling Lord Literistic for guiding me through the process, and to John Flicker, Jessica Waters, Dennis Ambrose, and Michelle Daniel at Random House/Bantam Books for their editorial support. Thanks to Bruce Riedel for his long friendship and wise counsel. Thanks to Plato Cacheris for having my back when I went public that the CIA had waterboarded prisoners. And most of all, thanks to "Katherine." I don't know what I did to deserve a wife as wonderful as you.

One preemptive apology: Any errors, faulty recollections, or oversights that appear in this book are mine and mine alone. I have related the facts as I recall them, or as the CIA has allowed me to tell them, but there are bound to be some mistakes. For those I take full responsibility.

ABOUT THE AUTHOR

JOHN KIRIAKOU is a senior staff member in the United States Senate. He served in the Central Intelligence Agency from 1990 until March 2004, first as an analyst and later as a counterterrorism operations officer. He was later named the executive assistant to the CIA's associate deputy director for operations, where he was intimately involved in planning for the Iraq war. His op-eds on the Middle East and Afghanistan have appeared in more than eighty newspapers in dozens of countries.

ABOUT THE TYPE

This book was set in Sabon, a typeface designed by the well-known German typographer Jan Tschichold (1902–74). Sabon's design is based upon the original letterforms of Claude Garamond and was created specifically to be used for three sources: foundry type for hand composition, Linotype, and Monotype. Tschichold named his typeface for the famous Frankfurt typefounder Jacques Sabon, who died in 1580.